Prosperity Simplified

Lifeonaire

Prosperity Simplified

An uncommon, in your face approach to wealth, success and prosperity. Be prepared to "unlearn" just about everything you thought you knew about success.

STEVE COOK AND
SHAUN McCLOSKEY

Published by Lifeonaire Promotions, LLC

Lifeonaire

Published by Lifeonaire Promotions, LLC
ISBN: 978-0-9863228-0-8

Lifeonaire Promotions, LLC
P.O. Box 471, Baraboo WI 53913
www.lifeonaire.com

Table of Contents

Acknowledgments 7
Introduction 9
A Note from Shaun McCloskey 11
Chapter 1 15
Chapter 2 31
Chapter 3 45
Chapter 4 91
Chapter 5 135
Chapter 6 173
Chapter 7 187
Chapter 8 231
Epilogue 265
Final Thoughts from the Authors 281
How can you get started? 287

Acknowledgments

I decided to keep this short and sweet. It is God who gave me the word *Lifeonaire* and along with it the burden of taking the LIFEonaire message to the world. It is through Him that everything good in my life can be attributed to. While many people have contributed to Lifeonaire in many different ways, I trust that it is God who brought every one of those people into my path. I am thankful for the abundant life that I have found through Jesus Christ, and I am thankful for the opportunities that I have been given to share it with others. And for all of you who have contributed to Lifeonaire in some shape, way, or form, know that I am forever going to be thankful for all of you. I hope that throughout my life, I can give back in some way all that I have received.

Introduction

This book has taken far too long to get to you. I spent many years working on it. In fact, there were four previous versions of the Lifeonaire book before this one; however, I always felt that each of them just weren't a good-enough depiction of Lifeonaire for me to attach my name. I spent years trying to get it just right. The truth is, if it weren't for the encouragement of my students, it may have never gotten to print. Thankfully, it was my students who reminded me that for every minute I wait to release the book, I was robbing the world of the impact that the Lifeonaire principles could generate. If it weren't for them, I'd probably still be working on it right now. Let me tell you how I finally came to the point of having a manuscript that I was willing to send to the publisher. Lifeonaire is something that is changing lives, and I tried repeatedly to put it into words. I struggled to get it to flow from one idea to another. In everyday life, however, I could teach people the Lifeonaire concepts, and they got it. It made sense to them. Putting it into writing was a lot more difficult. Then one day, when talking with Shaun, he suggested that I stop trying to write a nonfiction book and instead that we write a novel. He reminded me that the way we teach Lifeonaire is through telling real-life stories. Everyone relates to the stories we tell, they hit close to home. So, while this is not a true story as depicted from one person's experience, it is a compilation of very true and real life stories that Shaun and I have experienced both in our own lives and through the lives of our students. Don't be surprised if you are reading this and you think that something sounds familiar, because it may have come out during one of our teachings with you. As teachers of Lifeonaire, we're still growing ourselves. We learn new things every day, which means that this book is not the end; it is only the beginning. We may write other books on the topic, and we may update this one, but we'll always be teaching, and what we teach will always be based on real-life experiences that both Shaun and I have had the privilege of sharing and learning with our students. Enjoy the read. It is my hope and my prayer that it makes a tremendous impact on your life and those you care about. And most importantly, one that helps you to experience the abundant life that you were intended to live.

God bless you, Steve Cook.

PS: There is an important *free gift offer* from me on the last page of this book. This gift can make an enormous impact on your ability to implement the principles you're about to learn in this book and take your life to an entirely new level. It's also a way to continue our relationship beyond this book. Please take a minute right now to act on it. It's that important.

A Note from Shaun McCloskey

As I sit here contemplating you, the reader, and what the experience of reading this book may mean for your life, I can't help but feel as excited as a little kid at Christmas. Thinking back to when I first learned about Lifeonaire and started applying the principles into my own life, I remember being open to some of it, but truth be told, I also found myself resistant to a lot of the Lifeonaire principles at first. What you're about to learn goes against the grain of what you've likely heard or read everywhere else. We live in a world where we are taught that more is always better, busier always means more productive, and money is always the answer. It wasn't very long ago that I had more than I'd ever had in my entire life- I was busier (and in many ways more productive) than ever, and making more money in a year than I had ever imagined. And yet...I wasn't satisfied. I wanted freedom so badly I could taste it, and I was doing everything all the books said I should, working hard and making money. But I didn't feel free. I had glimpses of it at times, but something was missing. I'm honored to be a part of sharing this Lifeonaire message along side my good friend, Steve Cook. When he approached me years ago with this crazy word and the meaning behind it, I had no idea that it would grow to what it has become today.

Lifeonaire is changing lives all over the country. It has challenged what people, including myself, once thought of the "American Dream." But I've been privileged to see it change lives for the better over and over again. I've seen marriages restored. I've seen broken business-men and women starting over from scratch after losing everything, able to rebuild their lives and businesses in a totally new way and come out stronger. I've seen people grow up and mature in ways that didn't require them to stop living life or having fun. I've had older men and women tell me they would have lived life totally differently if they'd only known Lifeonaire at a younger age. I've seen young people pursue completely different careers than what they started out pursuing. I've seen people stop doing what the world told them to do and start doing what their own personal vision stated instead. I've seen people that used to work ninety hours per week now working just twenty hours per week and taking four months out of every year to travel and enjoy life. I've seen people quit their jobs to pursue their dreams and succeed! I've seen mothers, who never before imagined it possible, able to quit their jobs and stay at home with their children. I've even seen people come to know God. I've seen so much already, and con-tinue to see more lives change every day as a result of this crazy thing called Lifeonaire. The best part of all is that each person who embraces Lifeonaire chooses his or her own journey. Lifeonaire will never tell you how to live, or even what to do for that matter. But it has helped thousands of people figure out what it is they really wanted out of their lives, and then helped them come up with a plan to get there. It's amazing to me how few people are actually pursuing the life they truly want, including myself just a few years ago. It's even more amazing to me to see how few people even know specifically what they really want out of their life. Get ready, because all of that is about to change. Welcome to Lifeonaire. I'm truly excited for you.

Give first, Shaun McCloskey

Chapter

1

Alex thought his head might explode. *Here we go again*, he thought, *she just doesn't get it.*

"I don't understand why you can't do something with your son once in a while!" Kerry was visibly upset and quickly reaching her wit's end. "You spend every waking moment working. Justin hardly knows who you are anymore! Can't you take one weekend out of the entire year to enjoy some quality time with him and maybe, just maybe, be a positive influence? Pretend that you care about him?"

"That's not fair," Alex snapped back, now feeling offended as much as angry. "I work my guts out so that he—and *you* for that matter—can have the things you have! I put this roof over your head, I put food on the table, I pay for the ridiculously expensive toys that he has."

"Now *that* is not fair, Alex. *You* are the one who bought those toys and the guitars. Justin would have been happy with any regular old run-of-the-mill guitar, but no, you had to get him the most expensive thing in the store to feed your own ego. It's always about you, even though you try to pretend it's about us!"

This one was getting ugly fast, Alex thought. *Why didn't she understand?* What was he supposed to do? Let everything go, perhaps file bankruptcy so he could go on some stupid camping trip?

It was true. Alex worked a lot. *A lot.* But it wasn't about him, at least not in his mind. He honestly wanted the best for his family, and that's what he worked for. His heart's greatest desire was to provide a great life for his family. He was doing it *all* for them, and that meant long hours at work, most of the time. It wasn't supposed to be this way, not that it had started off any smoother. When he started his own construction company years earlier, Kerry hadn't been very happy about it. She'd wanted him to take a safer and more secure route in his career choice. *Starting your own business is a little risky isn't it?* she'd asked him. It had been more statement than question, even then.

His response had been that working for himself would mean more freedom to do what they wanted, when they wanted. Being the boss was always better than being the employee, right? She had given in, of course. Looking back, he realized that it was more that she'd *reluctantly agreed.* She'd loved him and believed in him, and at that time, they'd still been young and fresh, with their whole lives ahead of them—just a few years out of college and still wet behind the ears. He had promised her that this would be the key to their future. They would live full and abundant lives. Owning his own business had seemed like the icing on the cake of the American Dream.

Now, of course, it seemed less like a dream and more like a nightmare.

Between the long hours, meeting payroll for his crew, the hassles of permits, and the never-ending paperwork, he felt like he would never get caught up with work, let alone get ahead enough for a weekend of camping with his son. Every time he thought things would get better, a new slew of issues arose for him to deal with. He was only thirty-nine, but he felt and looked closer to fifty. Now he was starting to question how long it had been this way.

Kerry's complaints were coming at a time when he'd already started to doubt the direction his life was headed. He wasn't sure whether his doubts made her comments better or worse, but they definitely made him feel defensive. And angry.

"You know, if you didn't run straight to the mall every time you got upset about something, maybe I wouldn't have to put so many hours in," he snapped. This was below the belt, and he knew it the second it left his mouth. The expensive "toys" out in the work-shop and his "man cave of all man caves," which he just had to have five years back but hardly ever used, flashed through his mind a split second before the response flew back from Kerry.

"Are you *kidding me*?!" Her eyes were now burning through him. "You're going to compare a *purse* or *pair of shoes* here and there to the stinking *snowmobiles* and four-wheelers that just *sit* out there? It's one thing to blow the money on them to start with, but *you don't even use them!* At least I get use out of the things I buy. Besides, I put my time in too, and you know perfectly well that I'm not happy about having to work a full-time job. Maybe if you had a job that provided insurance, I wouldn't have to send Heather off to strangers every day just so I could spend all week trying to cover the extra expenses that *you cause!* The day care knows more about our daughter than you do!"

By this time, she'd picked up and was holding and trying to console the child in question. Heather, their three-year-old, had been crying on the living room floor for some time—since Alex walked in the door late again and this blowout started. She didn't seem very happy in Kerry's arms either, and the sobbing continued, making the already thick and combustible atmosphere even worse. Alex was quickly coming to the conclusion that the air around him would be sparked into an explosion if things didn't calm down soon. It didn't look like that was going happen, though, because Kerry wasn't finished.

"Have you seen the kids Justin has started hanging around lately? Of course you haven't, that would mean you'd have to be around him once in a while. *Your real* family is your crew and clients. You care more about them than you do us. I guarantee that you know more about them than you know about your own kids! Since you haven't been paying attention, I'll tell you. Justin is *not* hanging out with a good crowd. Half of those kids are going to wind up in prison by the time they're eighteen, and they might take our son with them! Are you willing to let that happen to your son just so you can make a few more bucks at work? Well, I'll tell you right now that I'm not!"

Alex started to feel sick to his stomach at that point, and it got worse as Kerry bombarded him with accusation after accusation, blame after blame, as if the sum total of all their problems was his fault alone. *This was a bad one*, he thought—not the typical argument that peppered their weeks with tension and discontent, but the kind that ended with them not speaking to each other for days on end.

"I never thought I would say this," Kerry pressed on, her anger swelling in her like a tsunami ready to engulf a small island, "but I'm not sure if I can do this anymore. I made a commitment to you when we got married, and I have stuck by it and stuck by you. But everyone has a breaking point. I'm just not sure that this is the best thing for me anymore. And it's not just me. I'm *more* worried about the kids. It's already like they don't have a father…"

The tsunami crested, and Alex couldn't decide whether it would be better to hide from it or try to fight against it.

"Do you even want to be part of this family anymore, Alex? I honestly don't know anymore. Do you *want* me to take the kids and go so you can get on with your business without us?"

The wave crashed down, crushing Alex and sweeping him out to sea in its wake. He loved his family dearly, but it was becoming increasingly obvious that they didn't realize it. Everything he did was for them—for their futures—but instead of seeing that and believing in it, they could see only that he was never around, more committed to his work than his family.

At least that's how Kerry obviously saw it—no telling what the kids actually felt.

Before he could say any of that, though, the defensive fight-or-flight anger that had always led him to the wrong place at the wrong time surged, eclipsing any feelings of remorse or fear of losing his family.

"*That's enough!*" he almost screamed, the last bit of control he had over his emotions slipping. He could hear himself, and he knew that he was on the brink of sounding like a madman. He also knew that he wasn't going to be able to stop himself. His control wasn't strong enough. "I'm not going to just sit here and listen to you put me down and threaten me like this! You do what you need to do, just figure it out before I get back!" He spun around and grabbed his coat, yanking it off the coat rack and knocking it over without stopping to notice, let alone pick it up.

Behind him, he could hear Kerry yelling, "Where do you think you're going? Don't you walk out of here like that! Alex!" But it was in the background, drowned out by the pounding in his head: the soundtrack of his own personal horror movie. He stormed out of the house, climbed into his big dually truck, and pulled out of the driveway, nearly taking out the mailbox as he slid into the road and threw the truck into drive.

He didn't know where he was going, but he knew he needed to drive. His brain was swimming with thoughts, emotions, and memories that swirled together in an unfocused pattern in his head. Whenever he tried to focus on a thought, three more forced their way through and wrestled for his attention, resulting in a tangled mess of thought and emotion. He had to calm down, he realized. He probably shouldn't be driving at all in this state. Out of the corner of his eye, though, he noticed the sign for the highway loop that circled around the city and as he headed toward it, he nearly ran the light that was already red and probably had been for some time. As he braked sharply, his brain ran even more rampant, thinking of all the sacrifices he'd made – all of which he did for his family, and yet somehow no one really appreciated everything he'd worked so hard to create. *How could she sit here and accuse me of not doing enough? Every thing I do, I do for them! All I want is for my family to be happy. All I want is for us to have a good life together. What does she think I'm trying to do? And yet, no matter what I do, it's just never enough. Is it, Kerry?*

Alex could feel the back of his neck getting hotter as the seeds of anger sprouted into full bloom in his head.

And what is this, the longest stoplight in the history of the world? There's not even a single car around, why is this light even red right now? Alex thought in frustration as he sat impatiently, fidgeting around, waiting for a flash of green that would seemingly never come. Fed up, Alex slammed his right foot to the floor and the tires let out a squeal as the truck shot into the deserted intersection. It was as if in this moment, nothing mattered. *Why do I even try? Why do I keep playing this game if I can never win?* Not even the fear of the criminal justice system mattered during this moment, as Alex's truck fishtailed through the intersection without waiting for the permission of a green light.

He veered on, picking up speed as he pulled onto the almost empty four-lane stretch of highway and settled into the second lane. Then he stared straight ahead, into the darkness of the night, and drove into the emptiness. In the back of his mind, he wondered if that was true of his life as well. It sure felt like he was driving into emptiness.

After ten or fifteen minutes Alex had calmed down enough to begin using his brain again, and the thoughts began to flow a little more clearly. He turned off the radio, which had been blaring since he pulled out of the driveway, and let the silence and the sound of the wheels on the road sink in. He'd always done his best thinking on the road and hoped that he could do the same tonight.

I don't understand. The thought ran suddenly through his mind, bringing with it the first hint of clarity of the night. He didn't understand, but at least he *knew* he didn't understand. It was a start. The next step was to *start* understanding. Had Kerry said that she was leaving him? That she'd already made the decision? No, he decided, that wasn't what she'd said. She had *asked* if he *wanted* her to leave. *How could she think such a thing? You would think I'd been unfaithful, the way she was acting.* He shook his head, wondering if that *was* what she thought. Did she think he was seeing someone else? Or did she just feel like he was cheating on the family with his work? There was something wrong, that was for sure. He needed to figure out what it was, and fast. On one hand, without Kerry nagging, he'd be able to get more done, and probably more quickly, but that wasn't what he wanted. The reality was that he loved her and the kids dearly. The last thing he wanted was to lose them. Everything seemed backward, upside down. He felt like he was inside one of those snow globes and someone was shaking his world around for their amusement. This thought, of course, made him angry all over again.

Had he done something wrong? *No, you've done everything right,* he told himself, half believing it. Marry a beautiful and smart woman after college? *Check.* Move into a beautiful house in the best part of town? *Check.* Own and operate your own business? *Check.* Have two gorgeous children? *Check.* Enjoy the finer things in life like nice vehicles and man-toys, never settling for less when you could get the best? *Check.*

It was true, though, wasn't it? They had two nice cars, a big house nestled in the middle of a quaint family neighborhood, and plenty of man-toys to play with. Justin had everything a teenage boy could ask for and enjoyed playing the best guitars available–not to mention expensive clothes, shoes, you name it. Even Heather wants for nothing. Granted, at three years old she's got a long way to go before getting the expensive toys, but still… His family had all those things, just about everything they could want, so what was it that didn't fit?

I'm so ready for an escape… maybe I just need to get away for a while, Alex thought as he continued down the dark, lifeless highway. *It's been a long time since I've had a vacation with just the guys. Maybe I can put a trip together and just get out of dodge for a bit and clear my head.*

Just as soon as the thought entered his mind he immediately realized that his problems would still be waiting for him when he got home. Although a trip would help him forget about all of this mess for a while, it certainly wouldn't solve the problem at hand. Plus, how could he possibly tell Kerry that he could some-how make the time for a trip with his buddies but not for a camping trip with Justin? Truthfully, there wasn't enough time to do either trip right now, and no trip would fix the problems between he and his wife anyway.

I can't do anything I want to do anymore, Alex thought, and *maybe that's the problem*. After all, it had been at least six or seven years since he'd gone on his "annual" guys trip. Perhaps this pill should have been a little easier to swallow since none of the other guys could go any more either, but the fact that they were in the same boat as Alex didn't make it any better. It seemed almost ridiculous that none of Alex's friends really made much effort to get together anymore. Everyone was too busy, apparently.

Everything I do is for my family and they can't even see it, much less appreciate it. I've even sacrificed my friends for them and it's still not enough. It's not like I plan on working these long hours for the rest of my life. I just want to make them happy... why can't I just make them happy?

Just then, in the quiet of the truck, it was almost as if Alex heard a voice outside of himself repeat his thoughts out loud. But this voice was different, not just an echo of his thoughts. It somehow discovered at least a part of the root of the problem too. As clear as the moon in the dark sky was illuminating the exit ramp ahead, Alex heard the word *"time"*. The word was spoken so clearly and distinctly that Alex was startled. Obviously no one else was in the truck with him, and a quick glance confirmed that the radio was still turned off. "So what in the world is "time" supposed to mean?" Alex muttered to himself. *Why did that pop into my head right now?*

Suddenly Alex remembered when he took Justin on a road trip to purchase a '68 Corvette a couple years ago. The car wasn't perfect by any means and needed quite a bit of work, but it was a numbers-matching car and he remembered how excited he was to start on this "little" restoration project with Justin. Had that really been two years ago? Where had the time gone? In two full years not an ounce of work had been done on the car. It sat parked in the garage day after day, just waiting for someone to shine her up and get her motor running strong again. Sure, he was still planning on fixing it up one day, he just hadn't gotten around to it yet. *At this point, I'd be willing to bet the car wouldn't even start if I tried to turn it over,* Alex thought sadly. The car had serious potential with a little bit of elbow grease. Alex knew it when he bought it. He got a great deal on it, and yet there it sat, two years later, in a lonely garage doing nothing but taking up space and collecting dust. Dismally, Alex realized that if he continued at this pace the car would never be finished. *How did I let two years go by? It feels like we just bought the car two weeks ago, not two years ago,* Alex cringed to himself, realizing for the first time that he may have taken on a project much bigger than he would ever have *time* to complete.

There's that word again... "time." Maybe that was a part of the problem. Maybe that was a big part of the problem.

There's just not enough time in the day! How am I supposed to provide for my family, build a successful business, be a good husband and father, do all of the things I have to do on a daily basis and still have any time leftover for me? If I had more money I could afford to spend more time away from office... Maybe I just need one really good deal to help put me over the edge and get me free.

. . .

Kerry broke down immediately after Alex's abrupt departure. She sank down onto the couch, crying, with Heather crying harder and louder than ever in her arms. Was this it? Had she finally reached the breaking point, the point of no return? And had she pushed him far enough that he wouldn't come back this time? She took a deep breath, trying to calm the sobs and pull herself together, but it was no use. *At least Justin isn't here,* she thought, as she hugged Heather closer to her, trying to comfort herself with that small blessing. Battles like this between her and Alex always upset him terribly. She was grateful he'd missed this one.

Kerry loved Alex dearly; there was no doubt about that. And she didn't really want to leave him. But she couldn't just sit by and watch her family disintegrate around her, like a crumbling building abandoned by its landlord. She could see the problem, but she couldn't figure out what to do about it. If Alex didn't want to accept responsibility for his lack of attention, she would move out with the kids and at least concentrate on making *their* life better. *A better life,* she thought. *That's what he thinks he's giving us with all these "things." Why doesn't he see that his time is more important than the stupid house and cars? Had she told him that?* she wondered suddenly. Had she actually said that she wanted his time rather than a new car? *Again and again.* She thought. But he didn't hear what she was trying to say. No matter how hard she tried, she couldn't make him understand. *Why doesn't he listen or understand? Why doesn't he care like I care? God, am I going to end up like my parents after all?*

·   ·   ·

Alex felt like he'd been driving for years, though when he glanced at the clock, he saw that barely an hour had passed. He'd made the loop around the city twice and didn't know where else to go. He glanced down at the gas gauge and realized that this trip would have to include a stop at some point, or it would end with him on the side of the road calling Kerry to come pick him up, and *that* was not about to happen. Not tonight.

Pulling over onto the shoulder of the highway, he turned off the truck, got out, and paced around to lean up against the tailgate. He stood there in silence for a moment, looking out at the black night. *There's got to be an answer to all of this,* he thought. *Why don't I know what it is?* Looking up at the stars, out of sheer desperation he muttered, "God, are you up there? This is Alex. You might remember me from last Easter. I sat in the back in church, so you might not have noticed me, but I was there. Anyway, you're all-knowing, right? Maybe you could help me out of this one if you have the time. I can't seem to get it figured out, so whatever help you can throw my way, I'd sure appreciate it." He paused, waiting for a sign or some sort of answer, and then snorted at himself. *Who am I kidding?* he wondered. *I think God probably has bigger fish to fry than trying to help me with a fight with my wife. He's probably on her side anyway,* he concluded, frustrated.

He climbed back into the truck and pulled back out on the road, deciding to get gas and a soda at a place he knew a couple of exits away. As he headed that way, he started to think about the people he did business with, and people that he interacted with throughout the week. *They don't seem to have all these problems. Why do I? I work as hard as any of them, if not harder. And I do better work than most of them. Why do they seem happier than me? Where exactly am I going wrong?*

Alex shook his head to clear it. His thoughts were turning circles, and that wasn't getting him anywhere. To distract himself, he turned the radio back on, and tuned it to the talk station that he usually listened to during the day. Apparently, the news talk he enjoyed was *only* during the day, though, because now the station had on some kind of church show. It sounded like a preacher in the middle of a sermon. "And hear me when I tell you that you don't have to live like that. God loves you and He is willing and ready to heal your situation if you will let Him," a man's voice was declaring.

Alex snorted at that and pulled off the highway and into the gas station, turned the truck off, and hopped out to pump his gas. *Well, preacher, let's see what you've got... I just asked for help ten minutes ago, so let's see how the Big Man works this one out,* he thought. He finished pumping, went inside, grabbed a soda, and paid for it and the gas. As he climbed back into the truck, he couldn't help noticing a coffee shop across the street that appeared to not only be open, but to be packed with customers. *How is it that a coffee shop parking lot is practically full this time of night?* Alex muttered to himself. While his first instinct was to simply get back in the truck and keep driving around aimlessly, he felt a tugging sensation urging him to cross the street and check it out. Like when Heather would sweetly yet firmly urge him to sing the ABC song "just one more time." It was almost as if he knew he didn't have much choice.

Why would a coffee shop be this busy on a Friday night? It's too late to just be the dinner crowd. I wonder what they have going on tonight, he thought curiously, starting to think maybe he should go check it out. The truth is, Alex was more likely to go to a bar for a cold beer on a Friday night than to a coffee shop. But this place was pretty packed and it appeared to be *the place* to be. Maybe it would be just what he needed to let his mind wander a bit, Alex thought.

As his pulled the 23 foot long dually out of the gas station, he quickly crossed the street and parked in the only spot available – directly in front of the entrance. If the last couple of hours were any indication of where the rest of the night was headed, Alex thought, this would prove to be a very long night. Although it wasn't in Alex's nature to only focus on the negative, he couldn't wait for this day to be over.

Chapter

2

Alex looked around as he climbed out of the truck and hit the button on the key fob to set the truck's alarm. This wasn't really a bad part of town—at least he didn't think it was— but you never knew these days. But it was a Friday night, and there were a lot of people going in and out of the coffee shop and hanging around chatting in the parking lot. The last thing he wanted to do is come out to his truck in an hour to find his custom stereo missing. He had just had the stereo installed 6 months earlier and he was really proud of it. The funny thing is, as much as he absolutely loved music and the quality of his new stereo, Alex spent so much time on the phone taking care of business while driving that he rarely got a chance to even listen to it.

With the truck locked up, Alex trudged slowly to the entrance of the coffee shop, the events of the day weighing heavy on him. He felt like a beaten man, someone who had given his all but just couldn't muster the strength to overcome life and all its obstacles. He was tired and lost, and he knew it. The problem was, he didn't know what to do about it. He'd spent the last year hoping that the answer would be around the next corner or through the next door, but it never was. *Just another day in paradise,* he thought wryly, wondering if life was actually *supposed* to be this difficult.

The aroma of freshly ground coffee welcomed him as he pulled open the door and stepped into the coffee shop. *This place is packed. Something is definitely going on here tonight,* he thought, glancing around at the crowded tables as he made his way to the counter to order a caramel latte. The sound of music and singing was coming from a section of the café that was just out of sight through an open doorway. The song he heard was vaguely familiar, although he couldn't quite place it. *Karaoke, great,* he thought, then listened more closely. No, it wasn't karaoke, he realized. There was live music going on—acoustic guitars, that was it. While the young man behind the counter was making his drink, Alex took a few steps toward the area where the music was coming from to take a look.

Through a doorway in the back of the café, he could see a small room with a makeshift wooden stage set up at one end. There were two people sitting on the edge of it, strumming guitars and singing. Their audience, mostly high-school and college-age kids, lounging on couches and sitting at small round tables, sang along with them. Alex glanced back at the stage, thinking that the two singers were familiar to him somehow. Looking closer, he suddenly realized that one of the men was John Robertson, the owner of Alex's favorite football team, the Warriors. He was a well-known public figure, a business owner who had recently purchased the local football team and turned it around into the national championship team. He'd been one of the city's top business people for years but had become a celebrity after turning the football team around and bringing the championship to the city.

What's the owner of a professional football team doing picking and grinning in a coffee shop on a Friday night with a bunch of kids? Alex wondered, surprised. His expression must have matched his thought because the barista behind the counter spoke up, "He does this all the time on the weekends."

"Huh?" Alex snapped back into reality and looked at the young man.

"Mr. Robertson," he replied, handing Alex his latte. "You look a little star struck, or maybe just surprised at him being here, but he does this fairly regularly. It's some kind of young people group thing or something."

"You mean like a church group?" Alex was even more surprised at this unexpected information than at seeing the man here in the first place. He'd read his bio, but he'd never seen anything about the man leading church groups.

"I think so," said the barista. "Or a mentor group or something. I'm not really sure, but it's something like that. The songs are definitely church-type songs. They seem to have a lot of fun, though."

That's it, Alex thought, suddenly remembering where he'd heard the song before. It was at some church something-or-other that they'd gone to. Yeah, he was pretty sure that was it.

"So he does this a lot, huh?" he asked, keeping his eyes on the stage and the crowd in front of it as he took a small sip of coffee. They were clapping, singing, smiling, and having fun. The whole atmosphere felt almost foreign to him; he never seemed to have fun anymore and had almost forgotten what it was like. For him, life had become about working, sleeping, eating, fighting, and working some more. Fun just didn't enter the equation. He looked at the joyous faces in front of him with envy, wondering how long it had been since he had felt like that.

"Yeah, most weekends lately," he heard from behind him. "He and Scott have made this like a regular thing for the last few months."

"Scott?" Alex half-turned back toward the counter.

"The other guy with him up there. Scott's been playing here for a while. Nice guy. They both are, actually."

Suddenly Alex remembered what he'd been trying to recall. "*That's* who that is! I went to high school with that guy! I knew he looked familiar. Does he work for the Warriors or something?" He frowned, trying to fit the two men together in his mind. What did Scott, his high school buddy, have to do with John Robertson, professional football team owner-turned-coffee shop songster?

"Scott? No, I'm not sure what he does. He has a lot of free time though, 'cause he spends plenty of it here," the young man said, trailing off as he walked to the other end of the counter to help another customer.

"Huh," Alex mumbled to himself. *The guy looks really happy up there.* For a split second, Alex found himself jealous of Scott and not even sure why. Scott did seem to have something that Alex didn't. The fraction of jealousy, however, was quickly overturned with sarcasm. *Maybe a little too happy.*

Alex realized his mood was being affected from everything that had taken place earlier in the night. As he realized the source of his sarcastic thoughts, he made the conscious effort to try to stay positive despite the fact that he really didn't want to be.

I wonder what it is that he does that gives him so much free time and keeps him looking that happy?

Alex turned away from the sounds of music and laughter and spotted a booth near a bank of windows in the front of the cafe. Winding his way around the tables and chairs, he reached the booth, where he fell onto the cushioned bench propping his elbows on the table and letting his head fall into his hands. His meager attempt to remain positive just wasn't working, and the happiness of the crowd was making him even more depressed. Instead of lifting his spirits, it seemed to highlight how unhappy he really was. True, he'd almost forgotten the events of the evening for a few moments, watching the people as they sang. But now they came washing back over him, and his anxiety level started to rise again. Why was he so incapable of finding the sort of happiness he saw around him?

Lifting his head, Alex reached for the menu on the table and turned it over. As he skimmed the items listed, he realized he hadn't eaten since wolfing down a quick breakfast at work. *And I got home late and missed dinner. Again. That's what started the whole argument with*

Kerry in the first place, he thought grimly. Suddenly he remembered a visit he'd had at the office that day. The memory only made him feel worse.

That morning, as Alex was sitting down to a rushed breakfast in the office, a mildly familiar face had burst in: Brian, the real estate broker from across town. *I've got to give Carol the speech about screening my visitors again,* Alex had thought, frowning. He didn't have time to see anyone who wanted to barge in. He'd set his bagel down and stood to shake hands, though, deciding to at least be polite about it.

"Brian, it's been a while! What brings you to this side of town?"

"The deal of a lifetime!" the real estate agent exclaimed as he popped the latch on his briefcase and pulled out a stack of papers. Alex settled back in his chair and willed himself to attention.

Brian spread several sheets out in front of Alex and pointed to one, which held a topographical map. "You see this beach?" Brian asked. Alex nodded. "Picture this there." Brian slid the map away to reveal a set of drawings, and Alex's mind began to churn. The building was absolutely beautiful and would bring a terrific price in that location.

Brian continued, "I've got connections on this one, connections that could turn this into the deal of a lifetime for you." He began to map out the details of a new waterfront development on the North Carolina coast—a really nice development, the kind that really brought in the cash. "Think about this, Alex. This is a

$500 million project. You invest just $500,000 and your profits will be in the millions."

Alex's mind was racing. He'd been part of big projects before, but nothing like this. This was huge. *This could be what I've been waiting for! Just a little hard work, and then I'll be able to take it easy for the rest of my life! We could finally take those vacations to Mexico, I'd hire some help for Kerry around the house, I'd make a few investments...*

"I wouldn't wait on this one," Brian said. "Opportunities like this don't come around often, and when they do, they're not around for long."

Alex snapped back from his daydream. "Trust me, I won't." A part of him knew that he should do his due diligence and actually research the feasibility of the project—and how much it would actually bring in— but Brian was right, and he didn't want to miss out on this opportunity. The promise of a better life was dangling in front of him, and $500,000 wasn't that much to pay for the chance to be with his family more often and give them what they wanted. He would have signed on the dotted line right away, but he didn't want to seem too eager. Nor did he know how he would come up with the cash.

As excited as Alex had been that morning after Brian's visit, he hadn't even been able to share the idea with Kerry. She'd been ready and waiting with the argument when he got home, and the night had erupted into chaos. But this deal seemed like it might be the answer to some of their problems, and he'd been elated to share it with her to see what she thought. This might have been the home run he'd been waiting for. He just had to figure out how to come up with the capital. Suddenly, Alex thought back to the two men playing on the stage. *Maybe they're an answer to my prayer. John Robertson is very successful, and Scott, who must be his friend, just pops back up from the dead after all these years? Hmmm...*

He pondered this thought for a few minutes. Certainly Robertson had the funds he needed, and he'd been known to invest in real estate and some other odds and ends. He wasn't sure about Scott, but if nothing else, maybe he was a connection Alex could use to get in front of Robertson for a few minutes. *Nothing to lose at this point I guess...*

Alex decided that he would try to get their attention after the "concert" was done and began to feel a little hope for the first time since storming out of the house tonight. Maybe he'd been led here for this very reason! He sank back into the booth cushions and got comfortable, hoping he wouldn't have to wait long. He couldn't see them from where he was, but he heard everything as clear as if he were sitting in the front row. He wished sourly that he had enough energy to clap and sing, the way the kids in the audience were doing. They obviously didn't have a care in the world. *Wait 'til life gets a hold of 'em.* As soon as they were out in the real world, they'd probably be just as stressed and unhappy as he was. He sipped his latte and tried to relax for at least a few minutes. If he was going to pitch a business deal, he needed to appear a lot more together than he actually felt.

. . .

Alex was deep in thought when he noticed that the music had stopped. The noise in the café had been cut in half, and he could actually hear individual conversations now. He shook his head quickly to knock the cobwebs out and sat up straighter in the booth, keeping a watchful eye on the opening to the other room but trying not to be too obvious about it. Within a minute or two, Robertson and Scott came out together, talking with some of the kids. He overheard just a few words and his heart sank.

"No, no, I wish I could, guys, but I promised my wife I would be home by nine tonight, and you know I don't want to keep Mrs. Robertson waiting," John said with a big grin on his face. He hugged, high-fived, and fist-bumped some of the youngsters while making his way toward the exit. Alex thought momentarily about chasing him down in the parking lot but then decided that was a sure-fire way to appear desperate. That was the last thing he wanted. Robertson disappeared out the front door of the shop and the bells on the door jingled as it closed behind him. *So much for that idea, Alex lamented.*

Scott was still there, though, laughing and talking with the group of kids. *Maybe I can at least get some inside info from him*, Alex thought. *Then again, he might be interested himself.* He made a point to keep looking in Scott's direction without staring him down, hoping that Scott would notice and give him an excuse to speak to him. It worked. Scott glanced his way, did a double take, and then excused himself from the throng of youth around him, walking toward Alex with a big grin.

"Alex, is that you?" Scott asked as he approached the table. He dropped his coat in the booth and held out a hand. "I haven't seen you for ages! What are you doing here? Did you come for the music, or is this just a pure coincidence?" Up close, Alex saw that Scott looked even happier than he had from across the room. Alex had been sure that when he saw him, his age would show more, but he looked youthful and vibrant. His own face, he knew, looked about fifteen years older than he actually was. He wore his stress in the sallow color of his skin and the wrinkles he'd developed around his eyes.

"Pure coincidence," he replied, shaking Scott's hand in welcome. "I saw you up there playing and couldn't place you at first, but then it hit me and I figured I would hang around and say hi. How have you been for the past…what is it, eighteen years now?"

"Yeah. Wow, I guess you're right," said Scott. "Since high school anyway. I've seen you since, though, a couple of times at church. Just haven't had the chance to say hi. I've been ushering when I've seen you and couldn't stop what I was doing at the time. It's great to see you now, though! How are *you* these days?"

Man, this guy is a little too bubbly, thought Alex. It struck him as excessive at first but then became kind of pleasant. It was actually a nice change, to be around someone who was in such a good mood even though the skeptical side of Alex was wondering in the back of his mind whether or not he was sincere.

"I'm doing great!" Alex replied, doing his best to match Scott's upbeat tone. "I'm in real estate investing and construction, and business is booming. Church, huh? I guess you've caught me on the right Sundays then. Honestly, with work being so busy, I don't get there much. I'm kind of a Christmas and Easter guy as bad as that sounds…" He shrugged, indicating the hopelessness of the situation. "So what are you doing these days?"

"Man, my family and I just got back from a trip to Europe a few weeks ago. It was supposed to be a two-week trip, but we were having so much fun we wound up staying for a month!" Scott was practically beaming. "Have you been across the Pond?"

"Nah," said Alex. "I can't find the time for trips either these days. Business is too good. I just stay busy with work all the time. How do you manage to take a *month* for a vacation? I can't even imagine that. I mean, I'm doing really well. I figure in about ten more years I won't have to work at all. So I don't mind working really hard today, knowing that I'll be able to kick back and retire soon. Right now I put in seventy or eighty hours a week, and it never seems like enough. How do you do it?" Alex couldn't believe he had just admitted his biggest struggles to someone he hardly knew. Where had that come from? Normally, he would have just talked about how well business was going and left it at that.

"Wow. Believe it or not, I can relate to what you're saying. I was like that just a few years ago. I worked and worked and worked, but never had a life. It was killing me, so I decided to make a change. For my own good, you know? These days, I'm loving life. I work about twenty hours a week, sometimes a little more and often times a lot less, and I get to spend lots of time on stuff like these get-togethers with the church youth group. It's a blast playing on Fridays with those kids. It hurts my head to even think about how my life used to be, with all that working and running. I felt like I was chasing a dream-" Scott's cell phone rang and he glanced down to check the number on the caller ID. "Hang on one second, Alex, I need to take this," he said as he excused himself from the booth and walked a few steps away to take the call.

Alex watched Scott walk away, bewildered by his attitude and outlook. He was really happy, glowing even. *Is this guy for real? What kind of a secret has this guy found?* he wondered. Scott said he barely worked, but he clearly had enough money to take a trip to Europe. How was he managing it? *Whatever it is, if this guy's not full of it, I need to find out about it. I want some of what he has!*

Now Scott was wrapping up his call and slowly moving back toward Alex's booth. "Yeah, don't worry, it'll work out. I'll be there shortly," he was saying. He stopped at the edge of the booth and put the phone back in his pocket. "Alex, I've got to run, a friend of mine needs some help with a personal situation, and I need to go meet him. It was great to see you, though."

"You too," Alex answered, a twinge of sadness coloring his voice. He hadn't realized it, but he wasn't ready for this little reunion to end. There were things he wanted to ask his one-time friend.

Scott picked up his jacket from the booth seat. "Hey, if you ever want to talk about anything or just hang out, I'm here a lot. I love this place so I practically live here," he said with a smile. "Stop by and say hi sometime."

"Sounds good," said Alex. "Maybe I'll do that when I have a free minute."

Scott laughed. "Well you've got to take a break before you wear yourself out!" he said as he started towards the exit. Then half turning back, he added, "Maybe I'll see you in church Sunday?"

"Yeah, maybe, we'll see." Alex watched Scott as he walked out the door, his mind going in a million directions at once. *Is this guy for real or did he just put on one heck of a front? I never found out what it is he does. Whatever it is, it must make him good money if he can afford to spend a month in Europe. How does he have so much free time? Why is he so happy? Whatever it is, I've got to find it. If I keep living this way, it's going to kill me. Something about Scott is different... and for some reason I believe he's for real. I think.*

******

So what do you think so far?

We would like to help you with your Lifeonaire experience by providing you with free tools to live it, share it, and experience it.
Visit the web site below to find practical resources such as a sample Lifeonaire vision, additional teaching of Lifeonaire principles, and discussion questions for personal study or a group setting. Go claim your free tools now.

www.lifeonaire.com/bookdeal

******

Chapter

3

Alex felt the stress of the argument with Kerry come flooding back as he neared the house, but he hoped they could get past it. He hadn't wanted to fight with her, and he truly needed her ear right now. He wanted to tell her about the offer earlier in the day and seeing Scott and the idea of approaching John Robertson for his business idea. Kerry was a great sounding board, but it was more than that. He wanted to keep her involved. He wasn't as strong without her, and he knew it. Though he hated to admit it, she gave him good advice and was extremely astute when it came to putting things together in a coherent way.

He pulled into the driveway and hopped out of the truck, thinking about what he would say. He hoped she'd cooled down enough to hear him. He thought for a moment that she might be in bed already, and although this would have been an easy way to avoid another confrontation, Alex knew that it would only prolong the inevitable. Plus, they had made an agreement years ago to try never to go to bed angry. They needed to resolve this.

Once inside, he found his wife sitting on the couch with the TV on but muted. She had a cable news channel on, though it was obvious that she wasn't paying any attention to the screen. It was just company, he knew, so she didn't feel all alone. She'd been doing the same thing ever since he met her. Heather was asleep by now, and Justin would be at his buddy's house until the next morning.

Silently Alex walked into the living room and plopped down on the couch next to her. It was his way of apologizing without actually using words, and he hoped she understood. He was sorry. He hated fighting with her, but it was hard to listen to her criticize him when he didn't feel at fault. It was even harder when she brought up things he already felt guilty about, like she'd done tonight.

Kerry spoke first. "I don't want to fight anymore."

He heaved a sigh of relief. That was what he'd been hoping for. "I don't want to fight either, and I definitely don't want you or the kids to leave. I'm just not sure what to do to make things better. I want to try, I just don't know what that means right now. I need you to help me sort it out and make things better. I also don't think that this falls entirely on my shoulders." He saw her raise one eyebrow as he said this and quickly added, "But I know that a lot of it does, and I want to change what I can. I just want us to have a good life. Together."

"This isn't the first time you've said that. I've heard this all before, Alex," Kerry said quietly. Then she seemed to give in a little; perhaps she wanted to believe him this time or heard something new in his voice. "What makes this time different?"

"I don't know," Alex said. "But I may have stumbled onto something tonight at a coffee house. I'm not certain, and I'm not even sure what it is. I need to talk to you about it. I need you to help me sort it out, see things clearly, the way you used to. My head feels fuzzy right now."

She snorted. "Your head is fuzzy? Are you sure it wasn't a bar you went to instead of a coffee house? What coffee house did you go to? Who did you see there? Were you alone?" The questions came shotgun-style now, the way they always did when she started to suspect something, and he held up a hand.

"Kerry, just hold on a second. I wasn't at a *bar*, and I wasn't with anyone else. I stopped to get a cup of coffee and try to figure out how to make things right with you. Let me think for a minute. It's been a rough night…for both of us. Let me sit here for just a few moments and collect myself, then I'll tell you what happened."

"Fine," said Kerry, a little impatient. "I need to go check on Heather anyway. You clear your head for a minute and see if you can make some sense when I get back."

Kerry disappeared down the hall, and Alex slumped back onto the couch with his head back, closing his eyes to think. He ran back through the events of the day and the scene at the coffee house, trying to decide how to tell her what he'd thought. *John Robertson, Scott, business deal, missed opportunity, singing, church.* Church? That hardly had any bearing on the situation, but the word had been right there—something he wanted to talk to her about. He replayed everything a few times before Kerry emerged from the hallway and settled back in to her spot on the couch.

"Okay, let's hear it," she said.

This time, he knew what he wanted to say.

. . .

Kerry listened intently as Alex began to recount his evening at the coffee shop, wondering if he was chasing another "deal of the day," that would amount to nothing more than another headache. Of course she didn't know any of the details about the business deal Alex was talking about, and frankly she didn't want to know. She heard enough about his work as it was, and she sure didn't need something else to worry about these days.

After listening to Alex ramble on about his ideas for about ten minutes, Kerry finally chimed in. "Sounds to me like you need to make a point to get back in touch with Scott and see if he thinks John Robertson would be interested in your deal. He's definitely a smart businessman—everyone knows that. I don't see how it could hurt, and it may end up being a big help." She sat back, knowing that she'd just told him something he already knew, and wondered how he'd take it. Was he going to ask more from her than that? Did it even matter what she thought, in the end? If this was anything like his other deals, his mind was already made up.

"I'm just not sure when I can make the time to try to track him down," Alex said, starting to sound defeated.

This change caught her attention; just a few minutes earlier, he'd had a trace of excitement in his voice—the first she'd heard in months. It was that trace that made Kerry decide to push the issue. It wasn't often that Alex got excited about anything these days, and she wanted to water that plant before it withered away. If he could get excited about something, maybe it would bring him back to life. Maybe he would become the Alex she'd married. The one she still loved.

"Do I have to remind you that you own your business?" she asked. "Just have your crew take care of your workload for a day. Put something off. You're the boss, *make* the time." Sometimes she felt like she was talking to Justin, having to explain how life worked. She could never understand how Alex—who owned the company—couldn't find time to get away from the office. He made the rules for the entire *company*, surely he could make himself a day off!

"Yeah, maybe…I'll figure something out. You know, I should talk to Scott too. I don't even know what he does for a living, but he just took his family to Europe for *a month* on vacation. He has to know something I don't. And he was *so happy and cheerful*. It was almost *weird*. He just seemed like he didn't have a care in the world. And it didn't seem like a front either. He really seemed to have something. I can't put my finger on it."

"A month in Europe? Must be nice. Doesn't sound weird to me, him being happy. If I got to spend a month in Europe *I'd* be happy and cheerful too," Kerry said softly, almost sadly. "I'm sure there are people out there who enjoy life *a lot* more than we do." She pulled her legs up on the couch in front of her and wrapped her arms around them, giving way to the fear and unhappiness that she generally tried to keep at bay. She looked into the distance, imagining her own family as that happy group, traveling to Europe for a full month, without a care in the world. She wished she could experience that, just once.

Alex hardly noticed her body language; he was still thinking intently. "Yeah..." he mumbled. "Like I said, I'll figure something out. Right now I've got to think things through so that I can get some sleep. It's going to be an early morning tomorrow."

That got Kerry's attention. "On a Saturday?" She frowned. "Again?"

"Kerry, I told you I had a lot to do this weekend. It's going to be the same for the next few weekends. Remember, that's the whole reason I couldn't go camping or whatever with Justin," Alex said with exaggerated patience, putting his head back on the couch like he was exasperated that she didn't remember what he'd said.

"I don't think that's the only reason," she said, standing abruptly and heading toward the bedroom. "I'm going to bed, are you coming now?"

"Yeah, I'll be right there, I'm just going to get something to drink." Alex walked into the kitchen and grabbed a bottle of soda from the refrigerator, twisted off the cap, and took a long drink. In his mind, he was imagining another conversation with Scott, where Alex was honest about how unhappy he was. How he was successful in his career but a failure in his personal life.

How he was feeling beat, burnt, and ready to give up. *I can't let him know the truth about what my life really looks like,* Alex thought. But what if he could help fix some of those problems? Maybe there was something to learn from Scott. It wasn't like they'd ever run into each other in real life—they didn't work in the same industry, didn't run in the same circles, didn't have the same friends. Maybe it was worth the risk. If Scott could help him find happiness, wasn't that worth making himself a little bit vulnerable?

As he lay in bed that night, long after Kerry had fallen asleep, Alex thought about the possibilities of what following this real estate "lead" could bring. He dreamed of a life with millions of dollars, bigger and better toys than he already had, trips around world, and being first in line for all similar deals. But there was a hollowness there that kept him from feeling truly fulfilled by the dreams. For some reason, those things didn't seem like the way to happiness. And there was something about this deal that made Alex nervous. He thought that he needed to explore that further, though he didn't know what exactly he meant by that. He decided just before finally drifting off to sleep that he would head back to the coffee shop—soon—to see if Scott happened to be there, and go from there. *Nothing to lose, right?*

• • •

The weekend was typical for Alex—visiting job sites, checking on progress and his crew, going over paperwork, and setting up his schedule for the next week.

He and Kerry hadn't gone to church in many months, and he hadn't seriously considered Scott's invitation in any case. He had far too much going on at work to take an entire Sunday off. As he worked through the weekend, though, the coffee shop episode replayed in his mind again and again. Each time he thought of it, he followed it through to a different possible outcome, ranging from the ideal situation of making the business deal that changed his life to abject failure and rejection. It was driving him nuts, and Alex knew he had to get to the coffee shop and meet with Scott before the fear caused him to chicken out completely. No matter how things turned out, he'd feel better for at least trying. *Nothing to lose, right?*

Tuesday morning came, and he decided that this was the day he would go by and see if Scott happened to be around. He would go there around lunch, he thought, using that as his excuse to be there, so that it didn't seem obvious that he was searching him out. Of course, he knew it would be a long shot, but even if he wasn't there, Alex could ask the barista when he normally saw Scott, so he knew when to time his next appearance. Either way, this trip would produce something, and Alex liked the idea of that efficiency.

He pulled into the parking lot of the coffee shop and noticed for the first time the name of the place: *Cup of Hope*. How appropriate was that? Sounded churchy to him, so he guessed that was why the youth from Scott's church gathered there. There were quite a few cars in the lot, but he didn't know what Scott drove, so it was impossible to tell if he was there. He took a deep breath, gathering his courage and headed for the door.

Spending the past four days anticipating this moment left Alex feeling both anxious and nervous as he entered the restaurant. He made his way to the counter, noticing that the crowd was a relaxed mix of businessmen in suits, college-aged kids in torn jeans and flip-flops, and families. He looked over the menu on the wall behind the counter and decided he was going to eat even if Scott wasn't there. He was hungry, and the menu held some of his favorite dishes. Perhaps this would become a regular lunch spot for him as well. He casually sat down at the nearest table while studying the menu, making a point not to look around too much, and doing his best to look like he belonged there. He didn't want to look like he was searching for anyone. Then he heard a voice from behind him, and he felt his heart beat faster.

"Hey, Alex!" It was Scott's voice, and Alex tried to look surprised as he turned toward the voice. Scott was getting up from the same booth they'd sat in the previous Friday night, and walking toward him. "What are you doin' in this neck of the woods?"

"Oh, hey, Scott," Alex said, striving to sound surprised and relaxed at the same time as he stood and shook Scott's outstretched hand. "Just in the area on business, stopping by for some lunch. How are you?"

"Fantastic!" Scott replied enthusiastically, clapping Alex on the shoulder with his free hand. "It's a beautiful day. Why don't you come sit with me while you eat?

I've already eaten lunch, but I was planning on hanging out for a while, and I'd love the company."

"Sure," said Alex. "What's good to eat here?"

"Go with the tuna melt," answered Scott. "You can't go wrong with that. Best in town! Let's go sit down and someone will come take your order."

Smiling, Alex agreed and followed Scott back over to his booth where they plopped down across from each other.

"Didn't see you at church on Sunday," Scott noted. "Did you make it out or end up working?"

"No, it was the usual long work weekend for me. Business is just too good right now." Alex replied, trying to sound like that was a good thing. Truth be told, he was also trying to dodge the church question since the topic always seemed to make Alex feel uncomfortable.

"Hi, I'm Dan." A young man approached the booth wearing a neatly pressed Cup of Hope shirt and baggy khaki shorts, carrying an order pad in one hand and a pen in the other. "Do you know what you'd like to order yet or can I get you something to drink to start with?"

Thank you Dan! Alex thought. *You just saved me with a nice diversion. The last thing I want to do right now is feel guilty about working instead of going to church... as if there's not already enough guilt in my life.*

"I heard the tuna melt is good." Alex said, looking up at the young man. "Is that true?"

"It's definitely one of my favorites on the menu," Dan replied.

"Sounds good. I'll have that."

"Anything to drink?"

"Yes, I'll take a large coffee with as much caffeine as you can scrounge up back there," replied Alex. *I could really use a pick me up right now*, he thought, although he was already feeling a little jittery. It seemed he couldn't get through the days anymore without drinking at least a pot of coffee, a couple caffeinated sodas and sometimes even an energy drink. "Maybe you could just hook up an I.V. and shoot it directly into my bloodstream."

Scott and Dan both laughed.

"I'll see what I can do. Scott, you still doing okay?"

"I'm just fine, thanks," replied Scott.

"Ok, I'll get this right out then," said Dan as he hurried off with Alex's order.

The two men made small talk until Alex's lunch arrived, and he decided it was time to steer the conversation toward something more interesting.

"So how was your weekend?" Alex said, taking a huge bite of his sandwich.

"Really good," Scott beamed. "Lots of family time and relaxing." He looked relaxed. Not like he was *trying* to look relaxed, Alex observed, but like he really didn't have anything at all weighing on his shoulders. It was a look that Alex envied.

"Must be nice," Alex replied, swallowing. "Tell me, Scott, what exactly do you *do* that gives you so much free time but still allows you to take month-long European vacations? I mean, I work my butt off, but I can't ever seem to find the time for the family, much less vacation. I would love to know your secret. I would really like to grow my business more, and if you've done it, I'd love to know how!"

Scott studied Alex for a second or two, and instead of answering the question, he replied with a question of his own. "Why do you want to grow your business more?"

Alex was taken aback. "Why? I thought I just told you why. So I can work less and make more. Isn't that what everyone wants? I want prosperity as much as the next guy, but sometimes I feel like I'm going about it the wrong way, because the *better* I do, the tougher things *get*. But you seem like you've got it figured out. So what's your secret?" Alex smiled, trying to act like he was making a joke, but he gripped his napkin tightly in his lap. He wanted that answer almost as bad as he'd ever wanted anything in his life.

Scott looked thoughtfully at Alex for a moment. Then he chose his response carefully. "Alex, what's your idea of prosperity? How would you define it in your life?"

Again Alex was a little baffled by the question, but he decided to play along, assuming that Scott was getting to something important. "I guess the same as anyone else," he said, taking a small sip of coffee and setting the cup back down. "Having enough money to retire, pay others to do the work for you, *spend a month in Europe with my family*...you know, just not having to worry about money anymore."

"So if I made $50,000 a year, would you call that prosperous?" Scott asked.

Considering that Alex had signed checks for almost that much last week, his response was, "Of course not! That's just a nudge above the poverty line in some states. How could anyone consider themselves prosperous when they're barely making enough to eat and pay a mortgage?"

Scott pressed on. "So if I made $1 million every year, that would be prosperous in your mind?"

"A lot closer, anyway," Alex answered, thinking about what that kind of money could do for him. He toyed with the napkin in his lap. "Yeah, I would say that would be prosperity, for sure."

"Okay, now let me throw you a curve ball to get you thinking a little," said Scott, warming up to the topic but still looking relaxed. "Let's say I make $50,000 a year, but I have zero debt, I own my home outright, and I live fairly modestly. Let's say I can pay all my bills with $10,000 a year."

Alex felt his mind changing as he thought through the numbers, but he was still having a hard time with the low figures matching his idea of prosperity. He took another bite of his sandwich and chewed slowly.

"Are you with me so far?" Scott asked, after a moment.

"I'm with you, I think. Go on," said Alex, wiping his mouth with his napkin.

"Okay, now let's say I make $1 million a year, but I'm in debt up to my eyeballs and I really need $1.1 million to stay afloat. Is that prosperous?" Alex was starting to see where he was going with this, and it was like a light was coming on, although very dimly and very slowly, way back in the recesses of his mind.

"I guess not, but how on earth could you not be ahead if you made that kind of money? It would be ridiculous to be in that much debt when you're making that much," Alex almost snorted.

"That's a reasonable observation," Scott replied. "But let me ask you, and you don't have to give me any figures because I'm not trying to pry into your business, but how much more do you make today than you did, say, ten years ago? Is it twice as much?"

"Actually, more like four times as much," answered Alex, feeling a little rush of pride.

"And would you say that you have four times as much free time now, or that you're four times as prosperous as you were?" Scott asked quickly.

Alex had just taken another bite of his tuna melt and was listening attentively to Scott. Now he swallowed, sat back in the booth, and felt his world changing around him. "Not at all," he said slowly. "Just the opposite, if anything. I have less time and less free money. Kerry has to work full time just so she can get insurance since I don't get it through my company. And I'm always working. I never get to see my family, and it's becoming a problem." He realized that he was saying a lot more than he had wanted to, but it felt like a relief to say it out loud, like a burden was being lifted just a bit. Besides, something told him that Scott would understand what he meant. Something told him that Scott had been through the same thing and wouldn't judge him for it.

"So if you doubled your income from where it is now, what makes you think that your financial or time management troubles would be less, based on history?" Scott continued. He wasn't being pushy or nosy, but he obviously wanted Alex to come to the conclusion for himself.

Alex paused again and thought about Scott's question. His initial reaction to doubling his income was to think that he'd be able to pay everything off with that extra money. That last part of the question, though, "based on history," made him rethink that. It had taken him somewhere between eight to ten years to quadruple his income, but over that time he'd also taken on a lot more debt, bought a bigger house, and had the expenses of the kids being born and getting older, not to mention bringing on more employees and an entire host of other things. None of that had come instantly either; it was slowly acquired over time. Unless he won the lottery, doubling his income would be an overtime process, and his history showed that the time it would take to make that extra money would add extra trouble as well, unless something changed. "I guess I see what you're saying," he answered. "I guess I've never thought about it that way. It seems like when my income goes up, so do my expenses, and my need to work more, so if it doubled again, *based on my past*, it would kill me!"

Scott laughed a little at that and smiled. "Don't worry, I'll try to make sure you stick around a little longer, at least long enough to figure out what I'm talking about and pass it on to your wife and kids." Scott seemed to change the subject. "Alex, I've seen you in church a few times. Can I assume you believe in God?"

Seriously, hasn't there already been enough soul searching for one lunch? Alex thought, wondering where Scott was going now. He felt comfortable with Scott for some reason, though, and trusted him as much as he could with such limited time together. He'd known the man when they were younger, granted not very well, but he hadn't said anything so far that was insulting or ridiculous. Actually, he was making a lot of sense. So again, Alex decided to play along.

"I'm not sure what that has to do with anything, but yeah, I believe there's a God," he answered.

"That's good, because He believes in you too." Scott smiled again, and Alex grinned a bit at this. "Tell me, Alex, what do you think God wants you to have an abundance of?"

"Well, I'd like to say money, although He doesn't seem to be shipping it to my front door via UPS. But yeah, I do recall hearing some bible stories talk about God wanting us to be happy, maybe even *abundant* as you churchy people like to say." Alex knew that this was a bit of a dig on Christians in general, but he was clearly teasing Scott and wanted to lighten the mood of this heavy topic. Scott could see that Alex was trying to cover his discomfort with a joke and he smiled to show he was in on the joke. Getting back to Scott's question, Alex continued, "The obvious answer seems to be things like peace, joy, contentment, and happiness."

"*Bingo!*"

"That's good, because I want all of that as well. At least I'm doing something right," Alex said with a sense of relief. "I mean, I need more money too. More money would bring me more joy, peace, and contentment."

Scott looked across the table into Alex's eyes. "Would it really, though?"

"Well, sure!" Alex exclaimed. "If things weren't as tight, I could spend less time working and worrying and more time doing the things that make me happy."

Scott brought the conversation right back to where it had been a few minutes before. "But what about your history? Has having more money ever given you more time or happiness?"

Alex stared down at his plate as he began to get a bit irritated. *This guy has a point, but he just doesn't get it. If I just had more money, all of my problems would be fixed.* Still, he wasn't sure how much longer he wanted to keep going around this circle of thought. Though it was interesting, it was also starting to make him uncomfortable. Scott seemed to be saying that his entire focus on life was misled, and he didn't want to think that he'd wasted the last ten years chasing his own tail, especially after all the progress he'd made in his business. "I guess not," he mumbled. He began to dig for his wallet to leave a tip for his tuna melt. "Hey, listen, it was great to catch up, but I've really got to get back to work.

Dan, what do I owe you?" he asked as the young man passed by with a tray of drinks for a nearby table. Dan quickly handed the drinks to three young ladies working on laptops and hurried back to over finalize the check.

"This one's on me." Scott quickly interjected. "You can get the next one. We'll go someplace a lot more expensive!"

Alex laughed and opened his mouth to object when Dan spoke up. "Speaking of the next one, are you and John still meeting here for lunch tomorrow?"

"Yes sir, you know we meet up every Wednesday. Keep the change," Scott replied, handing Dan some bills.

"Cool, see you tomorrow then," answered Dan, thanking them and heading back into the kitchen.

Could they possibly be referring to John Robertson? THE John Robertson? This is my "in" for sure! Alex couldn't believe his luck.

"Are you meeting John Robertson for lunch tomorrow?" Alex asked excitedly, almost intuitively knowing the answer.

"Oh, you know him?" Scott replied, thinking it was the only explanation. How else would Alex have possibly figured out whom they were talking about?

"Not personally, but I've heard such incredible things about him, both as a business man and as a human being. I've always wanted to meet him," Alex said, trying to disguise his hidden agenda with curiosity and sincerity.

"Um… out of all the Johns in the world, how did you guess I would be meeting with John Robertson?" Scott asked, incredulously. "What, are you… stalking me?"

They locked eyes and grinned at each other, as if preparing for a contest to see who could outsmart the other with a witty comeback. "Of course not, but I love the new curtains you just put up in your living room!" replied Alex. "I'm just kidding… actually I saw the two of you playing guitar here last Friday night, remember? I couldn't help but notice him on stage with you because, even though I haven't met him personally, I've developed a lot of respect for him over the years. I mean, c'mon, everyone knows John Robertson! It's not hard to notice such an influential guy like that in a small little coffee shop like this.

"Okay, it's all making sense now," Scott said, digesting this information. "I sometimes forget how many people he's influenced over the years because I've been working with him for so long. John is a great guy and is a very different man today than he was just a few years ago. Would you like me to make an introduction? Maybe you could join us for lunch tomorrow," he suggested.

Did he really just say that? Alex thought disbelievingly. *Maybe God is listening after all! And is Scott actually working for John? Is that where he gets all of his money? No wonder! But wait… how does he get John to give him a month off to go to Europe?* The unanswered but assumptive questions were flowing through Alex's mind faster than the coffee dispenser behind the counter.

"If it's not too much trouble, I'd love to meet him," replied Alex, wanting to jump up and down like a kid on a trampoline. On one hand, Alex knew his schedule the next day was packed with appointments with contractors, and rescheduling would end up adding a ton more work to his load. But he also knew that this could be his one shot, his one opportunity to make a good impression on John and turn an otherwise dead deal into the moneymaking opportunity of a lifetime.

"Great, why don't you plan on meeting me here a little early and we can catch up on a few things before he gets here. How does noon sound?" Scott asked.

"Sounds good to me! I really appreciate the invitation. You're sure I'm not overstepping any boundaries here?" replied Alex.

"Of course not, I wouldn't have invited you if I didn't mean it." Scott replied. "But I do have one condition for the introduction."

Oh great… I knew it… here comes the catch…

"I know you have a lot of work to do today, so your only condition is to try to have as much fun as you can today while doing it, ok? Deal?"

Alex breathed a sigh of relief. "Got it. Will do. See you tomorrow."

. . .

After spending the rest of the day in the office, Alex strolled in the door of his house just before 9:00 PM, missing dinner with the family again. He was more than a little distracted as he approached the breakfast bar to sit down and eat the cold meal that Kerry had left for him. He didn't even acknowledge his wife as she came in the kitchen and inquired about his day.

"Is there something special on your mind, or are you just not wanting to talk to me?" Kerry asked, only half joking.

"Huh? Oh, I'm sorry," said Alex. "Yeah, I'm thinking about a lot of things. Nothing bad," he said quickly, looking up at her. He didn't want her assuming that he was thinking about their fight the other day or anything else to do with the family. At least not directly. "I saw Scott again today," he added, taking a bite of the cold pork chop on his plate.

"What? Why didn't you tell me?" Kerry asked with more than a hint of excitement in her voice. Then, seeming to realize that she may have come across as fussing at him, she continued in a more subdued voice, "So how did *that* go? Was it a good meeting?"

"I said I saw Scott, I didn't say I *met* with him," Alex said. Then he added, "I guess it was kind of a meeting, though. One of the strangest meetings I've ever been in."

"That good, huh?" Kerry asked reluctantly. "I'm sorry. Was John Robertson there?" There was a kind of hope in her voice, as if she wondered if the "meeting" had anything to do with Alex's business deals. Alex found that odd, considering how disinterested she'd been when he told her about that business deal.

He shook his head. "No, just Scott and me. I went by that coffee shop for lunch, and he was there, so I sat with him while I ate. I *am* supposed to meet with him *again* tomorrow though. He and Robertson." A small smile came across his face as he thought about the fact that he would be able to talk to Robertson about business within twenty-four hours. He wasn't sure what he was going to say, but this felt like the chance he'd been waiting for.

"Honey! That's great! Did Scott set that up for you?" Kerry was excited, partly because of the meeting, but more because Alex was smiling, which was a welcome sight.

"In a way. They were already getting together tomorrow, and Scott invited me to have lunch with them and even suggested we meet up before their meeting.

"So, what did Scott think of your business deal?" Kerry asked.

"I haven't brought that up yet." Alex came back to reality then and took another bite of his food. After swallowing, he looked back at Kerry thoughtfully. "Kerry, if I asked you what prosperity meant to you, what would you say?"

Kerry was very confused now and gave herself time by pouring a glass of iced tea for herself and then one for Alex. "Um, I don't know, why would you ask me that? What did you guys talk about today?"

"Just humor me," Alex said. "Come on. What does prosperity mean to you?"

"I guess having enough money to do what you want when you want," Kerry answered with a shrug of her shoulders. "Now what? What did you talk about today?"

"I'm not totally sure, actually," Alex said cryptically. "Food, church, prosperity, God, lots of things I guess. Scott did have some interesting points, though. He made me think about some things a little bit differently."

"Seems like more than a little bit," Kerry said. "It's obviously enough to make you think about it all day and into tonight. Do you not want to talk about it or something?"

"No, that's not it at all. It's just that I'm not used to thinking about these things, and I'm not really sure what to think about them exactly. They present a whole different idea of life than I've...well, they would mean that I hadn't been doing things right, that's for sure. Let's get this cleaned up and go sit down, maybe you can help me sort things out. *Again.*" He smiled at this, and Kerry smiled back, more than willing to play along with this conversation if it was putting him in a good mood. This made Alex even happier. Maybe they were going to have a real conversation at last. It might be about something he didn't understand, but at least it wasn't fighting.

• • •

As they settled themselves on the couch, Alex recounted to Kerry his conversation with Scott, word for word. Kerry was starting to think that maybe they needed to invite Scott over, considering the effect he'd been having on Alex. This was the second night in a week that Alex had come home wanting to talk to her after getting together with Scott. It almost reminded her of when they were young and they'd spent night after night talking about anything and everything. If Scott proved himself to be a positive influence, she'd have to have him over for dinner. And often. She would wait, though, to make sure that he was the real deal. The last thing they needed right now was anything else negative in their lives.

Alex spent the next ten minutes or so rambling on about everything he and Scott had discussed and what he'd thought about it. Kerry sensed something different in his voice—excitement, but also a sense of confusion. Still, she welcomed the ramblings—they hadn't spoken like this in a long time. And if Alex was confused and coming to her for advice, she'd happily give it.

"So after hearing all of that, what do you think?" Alex asked after finishing his tale.

"Hmm, well it makes sense I guess, but I'm not sure exactly how it fits into your business deals or how it makes us more money. I mean… all of this is great but what we need is more money so that our business can run without you being the one doing everything all the time, right?" Kerry answered, thinking through her words. "After hearing all that, though, I think I would change my answer on prosperity just a bit, to go back to your question from earlier. To be more specific, I'd say that prosperity means having the freedom to live life. Right now we sure don't have freedom. We make a lot of money by most peoples standards, but we've also got a lot of chains on us weighing us down."

"That's kind of where I wound up too. I think that must be the point Scott was trying to get across, that the money is a tool, not the goal." Alex couldn't believe this just came out of his own mouth. Could there be any truth to this? *Maybe Scott was right… maybe I have been pursuing the wrong thing?*

"So I assume you're going tomorrow to meet John Robertson so you can get on with this whole new thought process and get us free?" Kerry asked, smiling, eyebrows raised.

"Actually, I don't know what I'm going to say to him." Alex shook his head, surprised at himself. "But I'm not missing that opportunity again. He might just be the key to us getting ahead. You know, I didn't tell you this because it seemed kind of silly, and I wasn't really being serious at the time anyway, but Friday night before I got to the coffee house I was talking to God and…"

"I'm sorry, you were doing *what?* Like, praying? Since when do you stop to pray outside of Christmas at church?" Kerry looked surprised but not in an unpleasant way.

"Well, I was being a little sarcastic, mostly just kind of talking to the sky. I sure wasn't thinking at the time that God was actually listening to me, but now I wonder if He actually did hear me and set this whole Scott and John Robertson thing up for me. It sure was a coincidence that I ran into them *that* night. They say He works in mysterious ways, after all." Alex said this in a kidding way, but Kerry could tell that there was a hint of wanting to believe it behind the carefree attitude.

"Honey, I don't know. I mean, I *think* I believe that God hears us and that He answers prayers, but I'm not sure if we're at the top of His priority list. We went to church, what, twice last year?"

"Yeah," Alex replied with a quiet resignation. "Christmas and Easter. Maybe you're right about that. I don't know. Still, it was a weird coincidence."

"Well, I'll agree with that. I think maybe that's enough pondering for one night. You go talk to John tomorrow and see what happens. That's all you can do at this point, right?" Kerry said, not wanting to get into too deep of a discussion. It was pretty late by this point. Besides, it seemed like Alex had said everything he wanted to say, and she didn't have any more answers for him. He was going to have to figure this one out on his own.

. . .

Alex arrived at work on Wednesday morning feeling like he never left the night before. His desk was covered with evidence of his late night, the stacks of paperwork nearly overwhelming. He sighed and brushed off a few crumbs then began to put the files back in order—or at least in organized piles.

Suddenly he came to something special: the "freedom file" as he'd privately dubbed it. It contained the information about the beach deal. He popped open his briefcase and placed the file on top, excited at the prospect of sharing this opportunity with John Robertson. This could be a real game-changer, but only if the man agreed to help him. He spent the next few hours checking things off his to-do list and then happily dialed Carol, his assistant, who answered in one ring.

"Carol, I'll be out for a meeting soon. Take all my calls and don't make any appointments for me before two thirty." He hung up then jumped as the "Kerry ring" chirped from his phone. "Hey, Kerry," he answered.

"You're not going to believe this."

It took just those few words for Alex to know that Kerry was fuming. *What now? Not now!* "What?"

"I just got a call from the vice principal at the high school. They caught Justin smoking outside in between classes."

"They...he *what!?*"

"You heard me. He was smoking. And they're sending him home."

"Have no mercy when you pick him up," Alex steamed. "He is *not* getting away with this."

"Whoa, hold on! I can't pick him up! I'm out of vacation days, remember?! Not that I used them for vacation."

"Well, I can't pick him up. I'm leaving to meet Scott and John in forty-five minutes, and I'm not going to let our son's stupidity ruin my chances at landing this deal with John!"

Alex heard Kerry breathe deeply, like she always did when she assumed her "argue discretely" voice. "In case you've forgotten," she said quietly, "you're the one who didn't listen when I told you I was worried about Justin. I told you he was hanging out with a bad crowd. But no, you have to wait until something like this happens before you pay attention!"

"I *have* been paying attention!" Alex hissed as he rose to shut his office door. "What did you want me to do? Remove his friends from the planet?"

"Be his father! What has to happen for you to see how much he needs you?"

"I know he needs me! Why do you think I'm trying to make this deal with John?"

Kerry groaned in exasperation. "I need to go. This is not over! Now go get your son!"

With that, the connection was broken. Alex slammed his phone on the desk then quickly shoved it in his pocket. He'd need to leave right away if he was going to do something—what, he didn't know—with

Justin, and still be on time for his meeting with John and Scott.

When he arrived at the high school, Alex was relieved to find Justin waiting in the lobby just inside the entrance. The meeting with the vice principal could wait. "Let's go," he said, giving Justin a look that left no questions about how he was feeling.

He dove into the truck and shoved the key back into the ignition, laying into both the gas and his son at once. "Smoking! Seriously, Justin, smoking!? I don't know where you get the idea that you can ruin your life when your mother and I have done so much for you. How selfish can you possibly be?! I'm so disappointed in you."

"It's just a cigarette. Anyway, I can explain—"

"Just a cigarette? You lost your right to explain!" Alex turned sharply down the road to Cup of Hope.

"Uh, Dad, home is that—"

"I know where we live!" Alex snapped. "We're not going home! If I don't make it to this meeting, I'm going to lose my chance to make one of the biggest deals of my life, and I'm not going to let you ruin it. You're going with me, and you are going to sit in that coffee shop and blend in with the furniture."

"A coffee shop? Awesome!"

"No, *not* awesome. Trust me, this is not a reward. Believe me, there's punishment coming, just as soon as I have time to figure out what it's going to be! Don't make a fuss, and I'll consider letting you leave the house before summer."

He pulled into an open space and slammed on the brakes. "Come on." He walked briskly toward the door, relieved that Justin was following him without objection. They walked in, found an open booth, and sat down in silence. Alex tried to stay composed. He needed to figure out how he was going to explain Justin's presence.

Five long minutes later, Scott walked through the door, and Alex felt his heart speed up. To his surprise, his anxiety went sky-high. "Hey, buddy!" Scott said, coming toward the booth. "How's your day so far?"

Even though it was still early, Alex glanced past Scott to see if John was with him but saw no sign of the businessman. "Good!" Alex blurted out. "Been busy as usual. You?"

"Every day is a blessing." Scott smiled back. "Who is this fine young man with you?"

"This is my son, Justin. I hadn't planned to bring him today, but I had to pick him up early from school. I promise he won't be in the way." Alex glared at Justin to make sure that would be the case. He didn't want him ruining this.

"The more the merrier!" Scott turned to Justin. "Nice to meet you, Justin. I'm Scott. I went to school with your dad when he was about your age." Scott held out his hand and Justin shook it limply. Scott then slid into the booth across from Alex and Justin. "John called me about an hour ago and said he wouldn't be able to make it today, something going on at his son's school that he didn't want to miss. So I can stay with you longer today."

Alex's heart sank at Scott's words, and he knew his face must have looked like his dog just got run over. But he tried to hide it the best he could. No use ruining this contact just because their first meeting hadn't worked out.

"Actually, since Justin is with you, let's play a game while we talk. Come on!" Scott got up and took them to a corner with two couches and a coffee table. There was a large bookcase against the wall nearby stocked with games and puzzles of all sorts to keep the customers entertained while they waited for their meals. Scott motioned to Dan, the same waiter as the previous day, to come over and then proceeded to order burgers and fries for the three of them. "That okay with you?" he asked Alex and Justin who nodded wordlessly. "Don't worry about lunch, it's on me," he continued.

Great, thought Alex, *nice consolation prize.*

"Justin, why don't you pick out a game while I grab us some drinks?" Justin shuffled over, but not before giving his dad a glance that said "seriously?" He looked quickly through the boxes and half-heartedly grabbed the one on top: LIFE. Then he walked back and gracelessly dropped it on the table. Scott returned with three sodas and they all settled themselves on the couches around the table.

Seriously? Alex thought to himself. *I really took time away from work and drove halfway across town to play a kids board game?*

Scott lifted the lid off of the box and father and son took the pieces out, begrudgingly. It had been a long time since Alex had played LIFE—a long time since he'd played any game, actually. He vaguely remembered this one.

After setting up the board and reviewing the rules, they began playing. Scott and Justin chatted as they played, but Alex's mind wandered. He could barely hide his disappointment over not being able to meet with John Robertson, though he did his best to stay focused on the game and look like a good dad in front of Scott.

Finally their food arrived, and they paused in their game to dig in. "Thank you, Jesus, for this food, I'm starving," blurted Scott. They all tore into their burgers, and silence reigned for a moment. When they started playing again, Justin got a card that told him he was going to be a doctor in the game.

"Sweet!" he muttered. "I'm going to be rich for sure!"

Alex, in the following turn, became a teacher. And then the moaning began. "A teacher? Come on, you must be kidding! I guess I'll resign myself to studio apartments on the wrong side of town and calling twelve-year-old cars 'new to me' for the rest of my life."

As the game continued, though, Justin struggled with holding onto his "money" as he had to pay for taxes, college, and other "life expenses" that popped up. At the same time, Alex kept commenting on the fact that he wouldn't be able to afford things like college for his children on the teacher's salary he was getting.

Scott had been closely observing the father and son as they played, casually glancing toward each of them but keeping his ears sharply tuned to every word they said. He knew that the words and actions from the game could be used for lessons at some point for both Alex and Justin.

"So tell me, Alex," he finally said, looking up at Alex with interest. "Have you given any thought to the conversation we had yesterday?"

"Actually I have," Alex answered, perking up as he recalled the conversation with Kerry the night before. "It kind of haunted me yesterday." He laughed. "I talked about it last night with Kerry, my wife."

"Good," Scott said. "I was hoping it would make enough of an impression to at least stick with you through the night." He smiled, looking cheerful and relaxed as always. *This guy is really comfortable in his own skin,* Alex thought. "So were you and Kerry able to define what prosperity meant to you? I assume that's what you talked about?"

"Yeah," Alex replied. "We talked about what it meant to be prosperous. We decided that it meant freedom. Having the freedom to live and experience life. Right track?"

Scott thought about this for a few seconds, and then answered, "Yeah, right track. But tell me, what does that freedom look like?"

"What do you mean?" Alex asked, confused again. Just when he thought he had the right answer, Scott threw him a curveball. "I mean, not having to work so much, or at all maybe, I guess. Being able to take more personal time."

"To do what?" Scott asked, digging deeper.

"I don't know." Alex was a little flustered that he couldn't come right back with an answer. He thought for a second then said, "I guess I've been behind for so long that I've never bothered to think ahead to what I'd do if I had free time. Maybe in the back of my mind I didn't really believe I would ever get to a point where it would matter."

"Good." Scott's answer made Alex frown, bewildered, as Justin sat half-listening.

"Why is that good?" he asked, more confused than ever at his old friend's odd way of thinking.

"Not good that you haven't thought about it," Scott replied as calmly as ever, "Good that you're *realizing* that you've never thought about it. Maybe now you will." He sat back in the booth like someone who had just accomplished something, but Alex was darned if he knew what it was he thought he'd achieved. He was getting more confused as they went on rather than more enlightened. And along with the confusion came frustration and some anger. He was definitely starting to wonder if meeting with Scott again had been a good idea.

"What good does it do to think about it if I don't have a plan for getting there?" Alex continued, thinking that maybe Scott hadn't thought about it that way.

"Good point," Scott said, taking a sip of his coffee. "Maybe you should start working on one."

Now it was Alex's turn to be confused again. Seeking distraction, he looked down at the board and counted off the spaces for his turn, landing on a trade salary with any player space. "Oh, look at this! I can trade my salary for that of any player! There's no question whose

I choose: give it up, Justin!" Justin mumbled something unintelligible and slouched on the couch in response.

Scott took his turn and landed on a life space. "Visit the Grand Canyon! Awesome! We went there with the kids two years ago, and it was one of the best trips we've ever taken. There's just nothing like it, and seeing my kids see it for the first time was amazing!" Scott was clearly psyched about the trip, and the opportunity to relive it through the board game.

Alex and Justin exchanged a glance. It was just a game after all.

"You guys ever been there?" Scott asked them.

"Nope," Justin muttered, looking at his father, who shook his head.

"Oh, man, you've got to get there sometime! It's worth the drive times a hundred!"

"Yeah," Alex agreed, "I'd like to…some time. But we haven't taken a vacation in six years, just a few weekend trips." And those weren't exactly relaxing. Between calls from work and fights with Kerry and the kids, Alex would rather have just stayed home.

He went for a swig of his soda and found his cup empty. "I'm going for a refill. You want some?"

"Sure—thanks!" Scott handed Alex his empty cup then turned to Justin as Alex walked toward the counter.

"So, Justin, what do you want to do after high school?"

Justin shrugged. "I don't know."

"Do you think you'd like to be in construction and real estate like your dad?"

Justin snapped to attention and made eye contact for the first time. "No way! I definitely don't want to do that." He had raised his voice enough that Alex, a few steps away at the counter, had no trouble hearing him.

Does Justin really have that little respect for me and what I do for a living? I thought he at least looked up to me a little... He slowly picked up the drinks and tried to put the nagging feeling aside as he walked back to the table.

"Here you go," he said, setting the refilled cup in front of Scott.

"Thanks, man! Justin, it's your turn."

Alex sat back down, trying to ignore what he'd just heard and make the most of the game. He didn't get to take time off very often, so he wanted to enjoy this as much as possible.

Justin spun the spinner for his final turn and decided that he would retire to Millionaire Acres since it looked like he'd accumulated more wealth than either Scott or his dad. After counting up all of the money, they found that Justin did in fact have the most money and had, therefore, won the game of LIFE.

They packed the game back up, and as Justin rose to put the game back, Alex held a hand out to him. "Would you give Scott and me a minute?" Justin nodded and drifted off, sliding the game back onto a shelf and sifting through a stack of puzzles.

Alex, with a bit of frustration, leaned in toward his friend. "Scott, you mentioned that I need a plan. What do you think I've been trying to do for the last however many years that I've spent working my tail off? I hope you aren't suggesting that I've been living my life aimlessly."

"Not at all, I think you've executed your plan perfectly," Scott answered, as calm as ever. "You're getting exactly what you've been striving for, I'm just wondering whether or not it's what you really want?"

"But...but we already talked about this. In order to get freedom you have to have the money to do it." Alex was losing this conversation, he thought. He wasn't sure whether it was a contest, but he was certain that he was losing. And the frustration was building. "Please stop talking in circles and tell me what you're getting at."

"Okay, fine." Scott leaned forward and looked directly at him. Alex felt nervous for the first time, like he was about to hear something he might not want to hear. "Let's take a closer look at the game that we just played. Who was the winner?"

"Justin won."

"What did Justin need to do in order to win?"

"He had the most money in the end."

Quietly but firmly, Scott said, "Isn't that how we all live life? We make decisions day to day on what will get us the most money in the end. We strive to become millionaires hoping to one day experience life at Millionaire Acres. But what if that day never comes? What if you worked your whole life to win this type of game and your life ended right before you got to enjoy it? Or what if you played this money game and didn't win because of things outside of your control? What if instead, the winner of the game was the person who had the best life experiences? Or, for me, to live a life that was pleasing to God. What if instead of spending all of that energy on becoming merely a millionaire, what if we strove to be a Lifeonaire. And with a goal of becoming one today rather than when we retire in thirty or forty years? Would you make different decisions if the winner of the game was the one who experienced the most abundant life?"

Alex was deep in thought. This made so much sense to him, but it conflicted with everything he'd ever been taught. He wanted great life experiences—that was why he worked so hard—but there was just something different about how Scott was presenting this to him. As if it was possible to have the life he wanted, without all the struggle. As if the great life experiences were what mattered, not the money. "I'm not sure if I'd do things differently. I *am* trying to live a great life."

"Look, Alex, you've been working hard for years, doing everything the right way, just like you've been taught. But you're not getting any closer to freedom or happiness. Don't you think you should have made some progress by now if you were headed in the right direction? *Some* progress? I'm telling you, you can experience a great life today, if that's what you're striving for."

Alex was speechless.

"Imagine for a moment what a prosperous life, as you and Kerry defined it, would look like." Scott paused to give Alex some time to think. "Now think about everyone that you know personally. I'm not talking about people you heard of here and there, or people you read about in a book somewhere. Think of everyone with whom you have a personal relationship–where you know what their life is really like, not just how it may appear to be from an outsider's perspective. How many people can you think of that are actually living that life of freedom and prosperity based on *your* definition?"

Alex was still speechless. No one was coming to mind, and therefore nothing was coming from his mouth.

"Can you think of one person?" Scott said.

"No, I can't. Maybe one, but no... not really."

"With all the people you know, you can't think of one person living the life that you would like to live?" Scott paused before making his point. "But I bet you're trying to attain abundant life by doing the same thing as them, working like a dog to make more and more money, when clearly that plan is not working out for anyone you know. And yet you're expecting it to work for you."

Alex sat back and thought about that for a few seconds. Scott was right. He should at least be *closer* to whatever his ideal was by this time. He didn't know what that was exactly, but he knew *for certain* that he was farther away from it than ever. And he couldn't think of anyone that he knew who was living the abundant life that he'd like to experience.

"Think about this for a minute..." Scott encouraged. "How many hours per week does the average American work these days?"

"Well, a full time employee typically works at least forty." Alex replied quickly, relieved to finally know an answer to one of Scott's questions. He draped one arm along the back of the couch. "But actually, that's not even true any more. Most people work a lot more than forty hours per week, either because they're required to or they're trying to get to the next level in their company or business, and you just can't do that in forty hours per week."

"Really?" Scott questioned. "You can't? Are you saying it's impossible? Or is it more realistic to say that most people typically don't? There is a difference, you know."

"Ok, I get that, but if you're in business for yourself, you can pretty much kiss a forty hour workweek goodbye—it just ain't gonna happen! It's usually a lot more than forty for me," Alex sounded almost boastful.

"Who ever said that a forty hour workweek *or even more* is what we should all strive for? I don't work that many hours each week and I have a great life!" Scott exclaimed. "And I know lots of business owners that have a great business and a great life and they don't work *anywhere near* that many hours either. Who ever set the standard that working forty or more hours each and every week is necessary? Do you even know?" he asked.

Alex shrugged. "No, I just always figured that's just how it is. As a matter of fact, the way I have always figured it, forty hours is the bare minimum people should be working. I feel bad, *guilty even*, if I only put in a forty hour workweek – like I could have gotten so much more done if I would have worked just a little more.

Scott nodded his head as Alex spoke. "You're not alone. But you should know that the concept of a forty-hour workweek isn't something that you or I consciously chose. It's been drilled into us for a very long time now, actually beginning way back during the industrial revolution. Yes, I'm referring all the way back to the 1800's." Scott gave Alex a half smile of apology for the impromptu history lecture. "The theory was that people should have eight hours of work, eight hours of recreation and eight hours of rest."

"Yeah, good luck with that concept," said Alex, sarcastically. "Even if I were to only work eight hours during the course of a day there would still be so much more to do. Just the drive time to and from my office is going to eat into my eight hours of recreation, not to mention all of the other things in life that require my attention or need fixing on a daily basis. So even if I did manage to only work eight hours per day, it's not like I would gain eight hours of recreation. That is, unless I just don't sleep."

"Well, maybe that's part of the problem," suggested Scott. "It's pretty hard to live a life of freedom and prosperity when we spend the majority of our time and energy focusing on things that don't necessarily give us more life. The thing is, Alex, we all have choices to make each day, choices that will either give us life or take life away. And our choices help us determine whether or not we can even win the game of life. The biggest challenge most people face is waking up one day and realizing they may have been playing the wrong game all along."

"Ok, I *think* I'm starting to get it, something has to give," Alex said slowly. "My way clearly hasn't been working, so what am I supposed to do now? Stop everything and just ask God to give me freedom?"

"That's probably the smartest idea I've heard from you yet," grinned Scott encouragingly. "But slow down just a bit, because you have to understand the importance of what you just said. I think you've got some soul searching and learning to do before you get there. How about I give you a place to start, and we'll just see what happens?"

"Fine by me," Alex said, throwing up his hands in mock frustration. "Give me *something* I can understand and work with. A place to start would at least be something."

"Okay, first of all, you have to understand that you now need to play the game of life by a different set of rules. The rules you've been playing with up to this point haven't gotten you what you're really looking for. Let's start with a principle. Don't try to understand everything at once, just go with me. The principle is this: prosperity equals abundant life. Repeat that for me and write it down." He handed Alex a pen and a small piece of paper from the stack on the table in front of them, nodding at him.

"*Prosperity equals abundant life,*" Alex said as he wrote it out on the piece of paper.

"Now write down this word. 'Lifeonaire'—L-I-F-E-O-N-A-I-R-E. It's like millionaire, except it means someone who is full of life. Prosperity is the freedom to experience life as we see fit. We need to understand what prosperity really means to us in a practical sense if we're going to pursue it. It's important that you know what prosperity and life mean to you if you're going to achieve them. Everyone wants to be successful, wouldn't you agree?" Scott asked him.

Alex nodded in affirmation.

"But what *is* success? Is having a business that makes a lot of money a success?"

"Sure." Alex nodded again.

"What if the successful business comes at the expense of a broken marriage or dysfunctional family?"

"I built my business for my wife and kids, I wouldn't want to do it without them," Alex answered slowly.

"Great!" Scott smiled. "Have you ever seen a magazine that features the five hundred most successful marriages or families in the country?" he asked.

"No, magazines always write articles about the wealthiest people in the country and their businesses, not their families."

"Exactly!" said Scott, pointing at him. "The world around us has defined success, prosperity, and integrity for us, and by default we pursue what others think we should have. We're not defining what we actually want ourselves; we're just following society's expectations. As far as I'm concerned, prosperity may or may not be an abundance of money, but it certainly is an abundance of life. It's not my goal to be a millionaire, but I definitely want to be a Lifeonaire. I want to be full of life. That doesn't mean that I don't strive to have a lot of money or that I don't like money, it just means that my priority—my greatest pursuit—is life, not money."

"But I want all those same things," Alex answered. He was listening intently, beginning to make sense of what Scott said.

"Is that what you're pursuing in your life?" Scott asked.

"I believe so."

"There's a slight difference in what you're doing and what I'm doing," Scott explained patiently. "You're pursuing money, in hopes that it will give you a great life. I'm pursuing life and am going to experience it whether I strike it rich or not. Scott paused and pursed his lips thoughtfully. "Since you said you haven't really thought about what being free looks or feels like, why don't I give you an exercise to do? I want you to take some time to think about it, then we can get together again and talk about it."

"Homework?" Alex chuckled at this. "Now you're giving me homework to do? Next you'll be calling me 'Grasshopper' and having me walk on coals like in *Kung Fu!*" Alex was getting a real kick out of this, but he wasn't against doing it.

Scott laughed. "Not just yet, *Grasshopper*. Here's what I suggest you do. Go home and talk with Kerry about prosperity and abundant life. You guys are one unit, not separate people. Sit down one night soon and write out a vision for your life together. Think big. Consider what you think a life of prosperity would look like to you, and put it to paper. Then give me a call and we'll have lunch again and talk it over. Here's my cell number." He quickly scribbled on a piece of paper and held it out. Alex took it and stared at it, not knowing exactly what to say.

"I don't know when I can get to this," he said. "I've got a lot going on this week."

"That's exactly my point," Scott said as he stood up, pulled out his wallet, and placed enough cash on the table to cover their lunch and a tip. "There's no reason why you shouldn't be able to make the time for something this important. You can't afford *not* to do this. I have to pick up my kids. Just call me whenever you get to it. I'm usually available."

Scott turned and headed toward the door, leaving Alex sitting on the couch like he didn't know how to get up. *Not what I expected from today's lunch*, he thought. *Not by a long shot.* He rose slowly, called to Justin and motioned toward the door, signaling that it was time to leave.

Scott, just ahead of them, turned back toward Justin. "Nice meeting you, Justin—glad you came today," Scott said sincerely.

"Yeah, uh…same here," Justin mumbled.

Scott turned back to Alex as he prepared to walk out. "See you on Sunday?" he asked expectantly, with one foot out of the door and eyebrows raised. Then he turned back to Justin. "Hey, Justin! How'd you like to hang out with my son Chris and me some time?"

Justin shrugged. "Uh, maybe…some time."

Alex followed them out the door without joining the conversation, remembering that he'd hoped to meet with John Robertson. In the end, he was almost thankful that John hadn't made it while Justin was with him. On one hand, he came hoping to put together the deal of a lifetime, only to leave with homework. But there was some excitement tied to the assignment he was given. Scott had messed up the way Alex thought about success, and it was both exciting and uncomfortable at the same time. It was different than anything else he'd ever considered, but something seemed very right about it.

. . .

After getting settled back into the truck, Justin broke the ice. "So this was your big meeting? I thought this was a work thing!"

"It was. Scott is good friends with a powerful man named John—the owner of the Warriors—and I was expecting to pitch a big project to him today."

"It all seemed pretty touchy-feely to me."

"It might be, but if it gets me this deal, it will definitely be worth it."

Justin turned his face toward the window and shrugged, losing interest. "Whatever."

Suddenly Alex remembered *why* Justin was with him, and his eyes narrowed, the good feelings from the meeting with Scott quickly receding. "I didn't forget about this morning, you know. I need to talk to your mother and the principal about exactly how we're going to handle your extremely bad decision."

The two fell silent then, and Alex slipped into this thoughts. *Prosperity equals abundant life*, he thought. After driving almost halfway home in silence, Alex finally spoke up. "Justin, let me ask you something."

"What?" Justin replied grumpily.

"The game that we were playing, would it have turned out differently if the winner was the person who had the best life experiences?" Realizing that he'd just asked a pretty deep question of a young man who was clearly in no mood for meaningful conversation, Alex decided to be quiet and go back to his own thoughts.

Justin didn't answer anyway. Alex didn't know if he was even thinking about the question. But he hoped so.

Chapter

4

Alex had left the coffee shop feeling overwhelmed, excited, and a little intimidated by the exercise that Scott had asked him to do. And although he was anxious to dive right in to it, he knew he needed to get a lot more work done before calling it a day. Since he had to take Justin home anyway, he decided to spend the rest of the day working from his home office, something he hadn't done in months. He found it hard to focus though, and his mind kept wandering back to his conversation with Scott.

Kerry was surprised but pleased to see Alex's car already in the garage as she pulled in next to it. "Looks like Daddy's home in time for dinner tonight, Heather!" she said to her daughter as she unbuckled the little girl from her carseat and helped her out of the car. "Yay!" Heather squealed, opening the door to the house and running inside, calling for Alex. Kerry gathered up her purse and followed her daughter inside, smiling.

After cleaning up the dinner mess and tucking Heather in bed, Alex and Kerry sat back down at the kitchen table to discuss the days' events.

"What are we going to do about Justin?" Kerry asked, sighing tiredly.

"I'm not sure. We do need to call the principal tomorrow; I didn't get to speak with him today. As for a punishment... a part of me wants to ground him for a very long time, and another part of me feels like it might be my fault."

Kerry looked surprised to hear Alex speaking this way and asked, "How so?"

"I'm not quite sure. My feelings are very mixed right now. I believe that I'm doing everything right as a father, but Scott really challenged me today. He messed up the way I think about things. He hit me hard with his words, and he got along with Justin as well as I ever have, if not better..." Alex's voice trailed off for a moment, then he took a deep breath and continued. "So what do we do? Ground him? I'm not sure how much that's going to help, but he needs to know that what he did isn't acceptable."

"We do need to let him know that we take this seriously," Kerry agreed. "What if we take away his phone for a month? I think that might hurt more than being grounded, and it would cut off some of his contact with that crowd. I can tell him in the morning."

"That sounds good, I guess..." Alex's mind drifted back to his time at the coffee shop, and he started filling Kerry in on the day's events, including the homework assignment that Scott had given them. As he did, he rose to pull a pen and paper out of a drawer and sat back down next to Kerry. He unfolded the piece of paper with his notes from the coffee shop and showed them to his wife. "Prosperity equals abundant life—that was the principle Scott shared with me today. He said that he wants to be a Lifeonaire, someone who is full of life, or something like that. He made it sound like that was the secret that made his life so great."

They sat together at the kitchen table, staring at the notes and the blank sheet of paper in front them and slowly began brainstorming what a life vision could look like. They weren't sure what they were doing and felt as though they were wandering in the wilderness at times; this was new to them, and they felt like they had very little direction. But they were working toward it.

"This shouldn't be that hard," Alex said finally, running his hand through his hair. "I have to do this kind of thing all the time for work, laying out proposals and goals and the tasks that come with them. I'm just not sure what I'm proposing here. What's our end goal?"

Kerry looked at him blankly. "You're asking me? You're the one who's been having these heart-to-hearts with your old buddy. I feel like I'm on the fringe of understanding what exactly the two of you are talking about, but I'm certainly not in the command center. You're going to have to get this ball rolling so I can help, or at least ask me something specific that I can answer."

"Okay," Alex said, "we're trying to write out what our 'vision' is for 'freedom' or a 'prosperous life', right? So let's start with the goal. What does freedom look like or mean to us? Give me some ideas."

"All right..." Kerry answered slowly. "Freedom is... freedom is...freedom is you not being gone all the time. That's the first big thing that jumps into my mind."

"Good," Alex said, writing this down and feeling like the first inch of the journey had been crossed. He was ready to pick up the momentum. "So in order for me to be here more often, what has to happen? More money," he answered himself, "so I don't have to work as much."

"I thought you said that Scott told you that one of the problems you have is focusing on money instead of freedom and life," Kerry answered cautiously. "But more money is the first answer you come up with?"

"Well, if I'm going to be able to spend less time working, doesn't that mean I have to have things paid off and enough money coming in to cover all of our expenses? I don't think I'm on the wrong path here," Alex replied very matter-of-factly.

"Yeah, I guess that's true," Kerry said with a hint of resignation.

"So now we have to map out how much money we need to get to that point," Alex replied, his business sense kicking in and figures already starting to work in his head.

As they worked through the numbers for the next half hour or so, Kerry had an uneasy feeling that something wasn't quite right, but she had no idea what was giving her that feeling or how to explain it. It just seemed like too many numbers and not enough heart, although she wasn't sure that would make sense to Alex. She didn't know what it was that was so elusive about this concept, but she felt like she had a little better grasp on the feeling of what they were doing, and though she thought that Alex meant well, she wasn't sure he got the whole "freedom" thing. It certainly wasn't his fault—he was trying, but this was really a new idea for him, and he'd never been good at accepting new concepts.

After about an hour of number crunching and discussion, Alex read back through the paper they'd filled out and mulled over the "plan" before him. It consisted of their current net worth, their outstanding debts, the current workload of his business, and on and on. It was a fine piece of business strategy, if he did say so himself! If he and Kerry were able to follow this, there actually could be a light at the end of the tunnel after all. Of course it depended on being able to make the money that was on the paper, and that meant more work in the short term. Something rang false about that—like it wasn't quite what Scott had been getting at—but he was sure that Scott wouldn't think he'd be able to change everything on a dime. There was always more work to do up front to realize big goals down the road.

Alex sat back and sighed, smiling tiredly at Kerry but feeling like they had accomplished a really big step in changing their future. Now he just needed to go over this with Scott and see what to do next. "Can you meet me for lunch tomorrow with Scott to talk about this, if he's available?" he asked suddenly, wanting Kerry to be involved with their life decisions.

"Actually, tomorrow is probably the only day this week that I could. I get a longer break midday, so I can definitely come if it's around noon." Kerry half-grinned, thinking that was a nice coincidence.

"Great, let me see if I can get him on his cell." There was a slight anxiousness in his voice and actions, though he tried to subdue it as soon as he felt it rising in him.

Kerry sat at the table looking over the sheet they had filled out. She still thought that there was something wrong with it, but she couldn't figure out what it was. However, successfully completing the plan—if they could do it—would definitely change their life. She hoped that when they talked to Scott, he could tell them what they were doing wrong. What it was that she couldn't put her finger on. What it was that was ringing so hollow about their plan.

· · ·

Of course Scott had been available when Alex called him and he quickly agreed to meet with Alex and Kerry at noon for lunch the following day. This guy was always available it seemed. It made Alex wonder all the more what he did for a living; he still didn't know, but he still thought that Scott must have inherited a lot of money, or was somehow sitting at the top of a large chain of command where he only had to make occasional executive decisions. That was the pinnacle of business ideals in Alex's head. An organization that ran itself, with only occasional input from the CEO, who collected enough money to be considered very wealthy. Enough money to do anything he wanted. But what was it he wanted, exactly? This was what he wondered as he tried to fall asleep that night. He felt like he and Kerry had put together a plan, and a good plan at that, but there was still something missing. His sleep was restless at best, that night, partly because of a new-found excitement and partly because of that missing piece nagging him. He finally drifted off somewhere around 4:00 AM. Waking up only two hours later at 6:00 AM, he moved through the morning like he was walking through water. Moving, but not at the speed he would like.

Alex finally started to feel awake with the third cup of coffee. That's when he started watching the clock. *Not much accomplished by ten thirty in the morning*, he thought as he sat in his office and tried to shake the cobwebs out of his head. He could feel the caffeine beginning to do its job and knew that he would be fine by lunch, which was about the only thing he'd been able to concentrate on all morning.

He'd just hung up the phone with Kerry, confirming that she would be meeting them at the Cup of Hope, when he decided that he needed to clean up his desk. Whenever he started to feel unproductive and unsure of what to do, organizing the last week or two of files, folders, and memos always made him feel better. It made him feel like he was accomplishing something but it didn't require his brain to be fully in gear. Alex picked up a stack of folders to alphabetize in his desk drawer and saw the freedom file sticking its corner out from the stack, begging him to not forget about it. Although he couldn't think about the details of that right now, it was enough of an impetus to start Alex thinking about when he would be able to sit down with John Robertson and go over it with him. Alex knew he couldn't let that opportunity slip away, no matter how much he wanted to work out the metaphysical meaning of life with Scott. This thought made him laugh to himself, and he knew that wasn't really what he thought of their meetings. There was definitely something he needed to learn from Scott. He just needed to discover what it was.

After half an hour of mindless paper shuffling, he glanced again at his watch and decided that he might as well gather his things and start heading toward the other side of town. It wouldn't take him an hour to get to the coffee shop, and it was only eleven, but he wasn't really getting anything done here, and the fresh air would help him wake up. A double espresso latte from the Cup of Hope would do the rest. Regardless of anything else that came from these lunches and meetings, he'd found probably the best latte in town at this particular coffee shop, and that alone was worth the trip!

In the truck and on his way, Alex rolled down the windows, taking advantage of the cool breeze and warm sun. The combination of fresh air and sunshine made him feel better and reminded him of summer evenings spent relaxing in his backyard with Kerry. This wasn't a usual thought for him, as he hadn't experienced that in couple of years, but today it was calling to him like a long-awaited vacation. The same way he'd felt as a child, when he walked past a swimming pool during a scorching July and wanted to jump in more than anything else in the world. That freeing moment when you found something that could bring both relief and supreme happiness. It was a freeing thought. Freeing...

. . .

The parking lot at the Cup of Hope was half full already at twenty minutes before noon, and Alex figured there must be a bunch of people starting their weekends early. His Fridays usually consisted of preparing for the work that had to be done on Saturday, and he was a little envious of those who actually took weekends off. Pulling into a space and hopping out of the cab, he made his way toward the door, hoping his new favorite booth was open. He headed for the counter to order a latte, noticing that the booth was in fact available off to the side and grinning inside that another little thing had gone his way. He paid for the drink and settled in to wait for Scott and Kerry to show up.

He didn't have to wait long, as Kerry came through the door no more than five minutes after he had sat down. He waved her over to where he was. "Do you want a coffee or anything?" he asked as she sat next to him in the booth.

"No, I'll just wait to order a drink with my food in a minute," she answered. "Is Scott here yet?"

"He should be here in a few minutes," Alex said, looking at his watch. "They have some really good sandwiches and burgers here. You should look through the menu while we're waiting."

Kerry reached for one of the paper menus wedged in a little metal letter-holder device at the end of the booth, and began to look over it. "Not very expensive either," she said as she glanced up and down the page at the different lunch offerings available.

"There he is," Alex said, taking her focus from the menu. "The guy in the shorts and a red shirt."

Kerry wasn't sure what she had expected, but Scott was a very unassuming presence. Not that there was anything negative about the way he looked. He was certainly well-kept and fairly handsome... he just didn't look like anyone special. He did seem very confident in his mannerisms, though; as much as she could tell in the twelve or fifteen steps it took him to reach the booth.

"Hey, Alex! And you must be Kerry? Pleasure to meet you!" Scott grinned at her, managing to look both exuberant and calm at the same time. He came across as self-assured and full of life to Kerry, and she smiled back, unable to help herself.

"Nice to meet you as well!" she answered. "I'm glad to meet the only person who's been able to steer my husband's interests away from his work, if even for a few hours." She smiled and wondered how this man had managed to direct her husband's attention away from work, which had been consuming him for years.

"Have you guys ordered anything yet?" Scott asked, sliding into the booth across from them. "I'm starving."

"I was just looking over what they have," answered Kerry. "Any suggestions?"

"Definitely go with the club sandwich on Friday," he quipped. "They always put extra bacon in it on Fridays."

"You do come here more than occasionally, don't you?" Kerry grinned. "Done—the club it is."

"Sounds good to me too," Alex added.

Scott grinned at them, but got straight to the point. "So, Alex, you two had a chance to sit down and work on your vision, then? I'm excited to see what you wrote. I'll go put our orders in, and we can start looking at it while we wait for the food." Scott scurried quickly up to the counter to place the orders and Alex looked at Kerry as if to say, *See, I told you this guy was full of life*, with an acknowledgement that he wanted what Scott had.

Scott was back in no time, and as he slid back into the booth, he said, "So what did you guys think of the homework?"

"I'm not sure," Alex answered for both of them. "It wasn't very easy, but in the end, I think we did pretty well with it."

"All right, let's see what you have."

Alex and Kerry glanced at each other, and then Alex opened the folder. He pulled out the neatly typed sheet and slid it across the table to Scott, turning it as he did so that Scott could read it easily. Scott looked down at the paper and studied it for what seemed like an eternity. Then he slowly lifted his head and looked at them for a moment.

"Tell me how the conversation went while you were doing this," he finally said.

"What? What do you mean?" Alex asked, surprised. "What do you think of the plan itself?"

"It's predictable, interesting, and not what I wanted you to do, but hang on before you start defending yourself because I'm not criticizing you," Scott added quickly, noting the change in Alex's body language. Scott could see that Alex was obviously ready to explain all of their numbers and why they made complete sense. "This is what I expected that you would bring me, and that's good because now I have a better idea of which way to go as we talk."

"What does that mean?" Alex asked Scott, glancing over at Kerry and seeing confusion on her face as well.

"Alex, you're not the first person I've discussed these kinds of things with. Surely you didn't think I would be offering this much advice and getting this involved in your business if I was just shooting from the hip. I don't mean I've got any kind of agenda or anything, but I've been down your road. I've helped a lot of people get from where you are currently to where you're telling me you really want to be. Maybe I can help you enjoy life a little more. That's all." Scott sounded confident and encouraging at the same time.

Alex and Kerry looked at each other for a long moment. Kerry spoke first. "Well, I for one would love to know anything that you can tell us that will actually help us live like Lifeonaires. Alex mentioned that to me and it makes sense. I want our lives to be better, especially if that means that I can get Alex to spend more time with me and the kids. Tell us what we did wrong on the sheet."

"It's not that you did anything wrong," Scott smiled at her. "If your goal is to accumulate the most wealth, sort of like the game LIFE, then what you did is perfect. But it seems to me that you and Alex really want to experience an abundant life, and you want it now, not many years from now. So if that's truly what you want, you need to change your thinking. Let's look over this and talk through some things."

Alex frowned, feeling a bit uneasy. The more he thought about it, though, the more he realized that this was no different than if he was teaching something new to one of his guys at work. Scott didn't seem to have anything but goodwill toward Alex, so there was no reason to back away from him until he saw anything different. "All right, Scott, where do you want to start?"

"Let's start with what your mind-set was while you were doing this exercise. What were you seeing in your mind while you were going through this? I mean, when you were thinking about freedom, what did it look like?" Scott asked.

"A full bank account and an empty bill drawer," Alex chuckled. Kerry smiled, but she had a better feeling for what he was asking.

"Us and the kids on the beach with no schedule," she said. Alex glanced at her with surprise.

"Oh, yeah, that would be nice," he said. He'd never thought about it, but that sounded exactly right. Looking at Scott, he asked, "Is that the kind of thing you mean?"

Scott smiled broadly and answered, "I think she's a step ahead of you there, champ. That's much closer to what I meant by visualizing freedom. Tell me more."

"Umm, I guess being able to be at home on the weekends?" Alex replied, looking at Scott for confirmation that he was getting the right idea.

"Good, much better, you're starting to focus more on your life," Scott said. He held up the piece of paper with Alex and Kerry's vision. "See, what you've given me here is what you want your balance sheet to look like. But I want to know what you want your *life* to look like. There's a big difference between the two. Get past the money part—that's only a vehicle to get you the life that you want, remember? Money is important, don't get me wrong. We'll get to the money part soon enough, but money is not life. When money is the goal of your life, that's what you will get, and life may not come with it. You said it yourself, You have four times as much money as you had ten years ago, but you don't have four times the life. Get it?"

Scott looked for a moment as if he expected them to suddenly realize what he meant, and that they were heading toward a glorious moment…but then the look was gone. "Okay, maybe not," he said patiently. "Try this. If you had no bills and all the money you ever needed, what would you be doing right now?"

The couple stared at Scott blankly as if he'd just read a technical manual to them in Japanese. Alex was trying to wrap his mind around the money part not being an issue, but Kerry was past that. She knew intuitively what Scott meant even if she didn't grasp the full picture yet. It was the mother in her, the natural instinct of protecting, nurturing, and loving her family. It was the same instinct that had caused her to question whether she and the kids would be better off without Alex around. It was an internal yearning for safety and happiness that had little to do with money.

Scott had had a feeling that Kerry was going to understand this quicker than Alex. He'd been excited when Alex called him and told him that Kerry would be going to lunch with them. Now he thought he saw a glint of understanding in her eye.

Alex, on the other hand, knew that he should understand what Scott was saying, but couldn't quite wrap his mind around it.

"Good question, Scott," he finally answered. "I guess checking to see if there was a ball game on TV."

Kerry frowned at him and rolled her eyes as if to say *typical man*. "I'm not sure what I'd be doing exactly, but it would definitely be something involving the whole family. That would be a nice change."

"It was for me," said Scott. "When I made my family more of a priority, it was a very nice change. Made my life a whole lot better."

Just then, their food arrived. Scott said a quick prayer for the three of them and they began to eat. "You weren't kidding about this club!" exclaimed Kerry, eagerly going in for another bite as the conversation continued.

Alex swallowed a bite of his own sub. "What you're saying sounds great, but let's get real. How do you pay the bills if you sacrifice work time for family time?" he asked, taking another bite.

"Well, before we talk about how to earn money or adjust expenses or anything like that, you've got to understand the *why* of the whole deal. If you take action on something with the wrong foundation or premise, your end results may not be what you planned. Sound familiar?" Scott asked in a gentle, parental way.

"Yeah, you could say *familiar* is the right word." Alex grinned slightly, understanding that this was exactly what he'd done for the last eight or more years. He'd been focused on the money rather than his family, and so he'd gained money, but not a relationship with his family. And he certainly had not gained a happier life. Perhaps he had to change his goals if he was going to change his life.

Kerry was taking it all in. Her interest was obvious, but she was processing things in her brain before she spoke, giving herself time to take it all in. Her perspective had shifted, even if only slightly, and it was showing her new angles from which to view her life.

"I'm not sure if you even caught what you just said," Scott continued. "You asked me about 'sacrificing work time for family time.' Doesn't that seem a little backward? If you're saying family is what's most important to you, what if you were to view things a little differently? What if, just maybe, every minute you spent working was actually a sacrifice of family time?"

"Well, it's not like you can just not work and live in a box," Alex snapped back, a bit stung by Scott's words. "I mean you have to pay for a mortgage and a car and food. If you're taking care of your family, you have to work to make sure they have what they need."

"I'm not attacking you or blaming you for anything, Alex," Scott said calmly. "Believe me, I've been in your shoes. Please don't take any offense, but your response is assuming a lot of things. For example, you're assuming you have to have a mortgage and lots of bills every month. What if most of what we've been taught about money was flat out wrong?"

"According to who?" Alex asked.

"You! When we talked yesterday, you couldn't think of one person who was living the life that you would like to live. Let me give you an example. I'm always going to use the Bible as my rulebook and foundation because I believe that it is actually God's word spoken directly to us. And if the one who made everything to start with wants to tell me the best way to deal with what He's made and how I can be the best version of myself, I'm not going to argue with Him. I'm not that smart. The Bible doesn't say anything about not working, though. Just the opposite, actually. It repeatedly says things like a man that doesn't work, doesn't eat and so forth. What the Bible *does* tell me is that my focus shouldn't be primarily on work or money."

"It should be on God, right?" Alex asked, trying to follow the conversation through to its natural conclusion.

"Yes, that's true," Scott answered. "But there are many other things that come before money too, like family and the people you love. People come first. Basically, we need to understand our priorities."

"So what, I just work enough to pay the mortgage and groceries, and that's it?" Alex wanted to know.

"Yes, let's get back on that subject for a moment. Why do you need to pay for a mortgage?" Scott looked at Alex and Kerry with a small smile.

Alex looked at Scott like he was speaking pure gibberish.

"Because I like having a roof over my head at night," he replied sarcastically. "That's a pretty good reason."

"I agree, a roof over your head can't be beat, but that doesn't mean you have to pay for it for the rest of your life or even that it has to be a place that you own," Scott countered. "Renting is cheaper usually, but I don't want to debate that right now."

Alex felt as though he'd just been asked to run around the parking lot, naked. "Renting? Why would I want to move backward in life? Renting is what college kids do, not families."

"Hmm, that's an interesting observation," Scott mused, as if the thought were novel to him. "Why, exactly, is renting moving backward?"

Alex was dumbfounded. Now Kerry looked dumbfounded too. Up until now, she thought she had a pretty good grasp of the conversation, but she was suddenly clueless again.

"Because owning a home is the American dream," Alex said, sounding a little exasperated at the line of questioning. "Don't try to tell me that it isn't, everyone knows that the whole ideal in this country is owning your own home, being your own person, individual freedom, and everything like that. It's why we fought the British. It's also smarter to own than it is to rent."

Scott chuckled out loud. "I think that fight was over religious freedom, not owning houses, but I'll double-check my history book," he said jokingly, trying to keep the conversation light. "But you just made one of my points for me. 'The American Dream'," Scott said, putting imaginary quotes around the phrase with his fingers. "Perhaps it has been distorted. The 'ideal,' as you just mentioned, has become the pursuit of life for almost everyone in this country. Life, liberty, happiness, peace, and joy aren't the pursuit any longer. Instead, homes, material possessions, and large retirement accounts have become the ideal. And we have enough of a track record to know that many achieve this, but few achieve life." Then he looked just a little more serious and asked Alex, "Tell me, who owns your home right now?"

"I do. Kerry and me. We're both on the title," Alex replied.

"And where is that title?" Scott questioned.

"At the bank," Kerry said.

"And why is it at the bank instead of in your records at home?"

Alex started to respond with a smart comment but instead stopped and thought for a second. "Because they hold the lien," he answered cautiously.

"Yep. Now, if I'm going to sell you my car, and you're going to pay me $200 per month for the next year, what happens if you stop paying me after ten months? Who owns the car?" Scott's questions were making a little headway; he could see it in their faces.

As Alex and Kerry thought about this for a second, Scott added, "Who still holds the title?"

"You do," conceded Kerry. "It would be yours, legally."

"Exactly," Scott continued. "So now tell me who owns your house?"

"The bank does, technically." Alex mulled it over, thinking about this as he said it.

"What's the difference between technically and actually?" Scott asked, aware that this line of conversation was finally getting through to Alex to some extent.

Alex stared at Scott, not wanting to admit that he didn't own his home. His pride wouldn't allow it. Yet it was the truth, and he realized it even if he couldn't see the bigger picture yet. After thinking for a moment, he said, "But that's just the way life works. People pay mortgages. It's like taxes or groceries. Nobody lives in a home for thirty years anymore, so the mortgage will always be there for most people, unless they're rich and can afford to pay for a house up front."

"And you would have to be rich to do that?" Scott asked him. "To pay for your house outright?"

"Well, yeah, by my standards. I certainly couldn't afford to do that," Alex answered.

"How much money did you make last year, after expenses for the business, if you don't mind me asking?"

Alex was reluctant to answer but wanted to give Scott this information, thinking it might lead into a conversation about his actual business and eventually lead to that meeting with John Robertson. It was one of his major goals in meeting with Scott after all. This part was just a bonus, although he was unsure at this point whether it was going to be helpful or painful. He hadn't even considered that it might be both.

"Around $200K," Alex told him. "It was a decent year last year."

"And how many houses in this city cost less than that?" Scott asked.

So it is about being poor to be happy, Alex thought. *He's going to tell me that my house is too big and my cars are too expensive. But can't you have nice things and be happy too? John Robertson's got that.*

"Plenty of them, I guess," he answered. "But sometimes in more dangerous areas or further from my work and the kids' school, so I don't know that the extra in gas wouldn't make up the difference. Not to mention the fact that I would have to find a buyer for my house, and with the market what it is today, who knows how long that could take." The barriers were thrown up one after another, but each one seemed weaker than the last.

"I'm not going to try to convince you to sell your house or anything else," Scott said frankly. "All I want is for you to understand what's real and to acknowledge that just because we do things one way, it doesn't mean that we have to. Decide what you really want in life. Consider me your high school guidance counselor." He chuckled at this, and Kerry and Alex both smiled as well.

Scott pulled a dollar bill from his pocket and laid it on the table in front of Alex and Kerry face up. "What do you see when you look at this?" he asked them. "Beyond a piece of green paper, I mean."

"Part of the tip," Alex answered, chuckling a bit.

"In God We Trust?" answered Kerry, more a question than an answer.

"You could get a lot of different answers from different people," replied Scott. "But let me tell you what I see. I see an employee who doesn't need sleep or lunch breaks. He works 24-7 without stopping, the question is just who he's working for."

Alex and Kerry pondered this for a moment, though Alex was beginning to see what he was talking about.

"Now, let me ask you a different question," Scott continued. "Was it easier to manage your house when there was just Justin, or is it easier with both Justin and…what was your daughter's name again?"

"Heather," answered Kerry, "and the answer is obvious there."

"I assumed so. So if you had two or three more children at home, it would be even more difficult to manage, right?"

"I don't even want to think about it," Kerry grinned. "Two is plenty right now."

"Alex, is it easier to manage a group of five employees or twenty?" Scott continued.

"Another no-brainer there, buddy," Alex answered.

"And I assume you would say the same about something like rental properties—the more you have, the harder it is to manage them all?"

"Yeah…" Alex replied slowly, trying to figure out where Scott was going.

"But people seem to think that the more of these they have, the easier it is to manage them," Scott said, tapping his finger on the dollar bill in front of them. "That doesn't make much sense if you see that for what it really is instead of what you want it to be." He tapped the bill in front of him again. "See, when you get deep in debt, what you have, essentially, is a whole bunch of rogue employees working against you instead of *for* you."

"I never thought about it like that, but I definitely see your point," Alex mused.

"You know the Bible says that the borrower is slave to the lender," Scott continued. "What does that say about everyone living under loans?"

"That's a little over the top, don't you think?" Alex asked. "To say that we're slaves to the bank?"

"Do you have the choice whether or not to pay your mortgage payments?"

"Well, no…I mean, yes, I could default on them, but…yeah, I pretty much have to pay them if I want to keep the house," Alex conceded.

"Any time you owe a debt to someone else, you are under their power, at least to some extent. And the more you're under someone else's power, the less free you are. Does that make sense?" Scott asked them both, trying to bring Kerry back into the conversation.

"But I've always been taught that there's good debt and there's bad debt," Alex countered. "All of our debt is for the necessities like our house and the business mostly, and the cars, which are all things we need."

"Try to think of it this way, just for the sake of this conversation. If you were to wake up tomorrow and all of your debt magically disappeared, would it be easier or harder to live a life of prosperity?"

"Of course it would be easier," Kerry chimed in now, "but…"

"I know what you're thinking," Scott challenged, "how are you supposed to have any of your nice things if you can't use debt to acquire them, right? Don't worry, we'll get there, but for right now you should simply understand the point that having debt very rarely leads to freedom. I'm not telling you debt is wrong. I'm just telling you that there are consequences attached to having debt and you need to fully understand these consequences if you're going to continue going down that path."

Alex jumped in, more challenged than ever by Scott's comment. "But what about the argument that says debt is good as long as the debt you take on is actually making you money?" Alex argued. "Take owning a rental property for example. If I go get a rental property and then put a tenant in the house, the tenant actually pays for the mortgage over time. Sure, I'm borrowing money to buy the house, but the tenant is the one actually paying it off for me, plus I get to make a little something every month." He sat back in the booth and spread his hands, shrugging a little. "This is a strategy that's taught even in business schools today."

"Well, that certainly makes sense on the surface," Scott replied. "And it certainly makes sense on paper. I guess it all depends on what your goal is. If your goal is trying to accumulate as much wealth as you can, that might be a great strategy. But let me ask you a question... is it possible to have a tenant in one of your rental properties miss a rent payment one month?"

"Of course it's possible, it happens all the time," retorted Alex. "But the idea is to keep it rented so that you don't have to worry about that. That way the tenant ends up paying off the house for you over time."

"I get it. No one ever purchases something with so called 'good debt' with the intention of things going wrong. No landlord ever buys a rental property with the intention of their tenant not being able to pay rent one month. But it happens all the time, doesn't it?" Scott continued. "When one of your tenants doesn't pay the rent this month, are you allowed to call up the bank that holds the loan on your investment property and tell them you can't make the payment this month because you didn't get paid from your tenant?" Scott asked earnestly.

"Of course not," replied Alex. "I have to make the payment no matter what happens. Either that, or the bank will take the house back and foreclose."

"Exactly," confirmed Scott. "And the minute this happens, you now have those dollars, those little employees working against you. When an asset, as you call it, has debt against it and things are going as planned everything is great. But the minute that asset doesn't perform as you thought it would is when you realize how much of a slave to the lender you really are. There may be degrees of how bad different kinds of debt are for you, but trust me, no debt is good. Debt is debt. And if given the choice, and if making decisions based on freedom and prosperity, it's always better to own something outright than to have debt attached to that same thing."

"Ok, that makes sense... sort of. But what about my own personal home? How in the world are you going to sit here and tell me it's better for me to rent a house than to own?" Alex asked, thinking he'd found a flaw in Scott's logic.

"I didn't say renting was better than owning. I just asked what was wrong with renting. I'm talking about debt. If you rent, you aren't in debt, even though you don't own it. You can leave whenever you want, unless there's a lease that needs to be finished, but even that can be paid out with a small fee. At least with renting there are no pretenses about who the owner is. But again, let's not get wrapped up in this argument. All I can say is this: if accumulating wealth is the goal of your life, then buying homes and things using debt may be the right thing to do. If experiencing an abundant life is what you want, then, perhaps, it's time to consider a different perspective and take a much harder look at your debt and how it has affected your life."

It was hard to argue with Scott, at least for Alex. He may have a hard time with some of what Scott was saying, but he was darned if he could find any holes in the logic yet. The only one he'd thought he'd found had been disproven almost immediately. "Ok, I'm listening," he said, not knowing much else to say.

"Another way to look at this is that money is something we trade in exchange for human labor. If you buy a house, you're trading money for someone to plan the design, dig the foundation, build it, wire it up, and on and on. Same thing when you get money for working—you're getting paid for trading your time or some kind of labor somewhere. In other words, you do something to get paid, right?" Scott asked Alex directly.

"Of course. If I could get paid for not doing anything I'd be all in on that deal, though," he chuckled.

"Me too." Scott smiled. "But think about this: if you're in debt, that doesn't just mean that you owe money, it means that you're required to do something to pay off the debt. That's called indentured servitude, at least that's what it meant back in the old days. Debt is a claim on human labor, so if you owe a debt…it goes back to the whole slave-to-the-lender thing."

Scott paused and must have seen their confusion, because he took a step back.

"Look, money is part of life, and it's a big part. Whether we want that to be the case or not, it's true. That might be why Jesus had more to say about money than just about anything else. When something is that much a part of everything you do, you have to understand how to use it. You've got to know how to master it, or it will master you," he said, sitting back in his seat like the conversation had just reached some kind of new level or drawn to a close or both. Alex wasn't sure. About any of it.

"You're saying the Bible teaches about money more than other things, like love?" he asked.

"Not necessarily. I'm just saying that it does recognize the influence of money on our lives and gives us the answers of how to master it rather than be mastered by it."

"I don't know if I'd say that we're mastered by money," Kerry broke in quietly.

"Don't make any payments on your loans for the next few months, and then tell me that," Scott's words were harsh, but he spoke them kindly. "Let me just say this. Money isn't bad, but being mastered by money is certainly not good."

"So you're saying that pursuing wealth is bad?" said Alex.

"It's not that building wealth is bad. Not at all. What I'm saying is that going into debt to do so sets you up in a cycle that makes it extremely difficult to be free at the same time. If you can't manage what you already have, four times more than you had ten years ago, it's likely that having even more will make things harder. You'll always feel stuck just trying to get by because you've played by the world's rules by default and didn't create a plan of your own. You depended on what you call good debt to move yourself forward, but the truth is, you feel less free than ever before. So really, you're sinking farther and farther into a hole, and you can't possibly make enough money to climb out of it."

Alex pondered this for a few moments. "Well, I can't argue that I feel stuck, and I can't claim that I had a plan—I still don't, really. So how do I get unstuck? I can't just give up my business—I've worked really hard to build it, and it does generate the cash we need to pay the bills. Seems like a good reason—"

"Alex, why did you go in business in the first place?" Scott interrupted gently.

"To make money and finally run things the way I wanted to. I saw an opportunity to make more and I went for it."

"Would I be too far off if I said that it was so your business could serve you?" Scott inquired.

"That wouldn't be far off at all, actually." Alex confirmed. "Although, I guess I haven't thought about it like that for a while…"

Scott continued with this line of questioning. "So, does it? Serve you, I mean."

Alex wasn't sure. He thought it did at one point… maybe…it had brought in more money than he'd had before. But now it seemed his business actually did little to get him ahead. "I'm not sure. It did at one point, but now I'm too busy with all the details."

"Would it be safe to say that it takes up the majority of your time?"

"Lately, yes." Alex wanted to spare himself from hearing Scott tell him what was finally becoming clear. He decided to speak up. "So no, it doesn't serve me anymore. At least not how I'd hoped. It just takes up all my time."

"Exactly!" Scott confirmed. "You end up serving your business because you owe it all your time. You trade your life—what you really want—for money. Your debt controls you because you have to keep working for the money to pay it off. Let me tell you what a mortgage really says because that will help to bring all of this together. When you decided to build your home, you didn't have the cash to do it, so you approached the lender. Basically, your conversation went something like this: Mr. Lender, I'd like to build a home for my family. However, I can't afford it on my own, so I was wondering if you would lend me the money to do so. What is the first thing the lender does to see if you qualify for the loan?"

Kerry answered confidently, "They pull our credit to check our credit score."

"Exactly! And why do you think they do this?" Scott asked.

"They want to make sure we really can afford the house, and that we have a proven track record of paying other people back on time," replied Alex.

"Right again. The lender gives you an application and thoroughly checks you out. What they're doing is trying to find out how good of a servant you've been in your past. In other words, are you a good and faithful servant to your lenders, or do you disobey your masters and not pay on time. The better servant you've been in the past, the higher likelihood of you getting your loan approved."

"Wow, I've never really looked at it that way," said Alex, looking at Kerry.

"Me neither," answered Kerry.

"Well, it gets better," Scott was just getting warmed up. "After the lender determined that you would make a good and faithful servant, they agreed to give you the loan. The documents that they had you sign essentially said something like this: If you agree to faithfully serve us with roughly 25 to 40 percent of your working hours, for the next thirty years of your life, we will put up the money and allow you to enjoy the use of this home. If at the end of thirty years you have faithfully served us as agreed, we'll let you keep the home. However, if at any point you fail to faithfully serve us, we will throw you out of the home and sell it to someone else. Oh, and by the way, if you do end up missing a payment and we have to throw you out, we get to keep any of the equity you've paid towards the property. And, of course, if there's *not* any equity in the home and you owe more than we're able to resell the home for, we legally have the right to sue you for the difference," Scott finished.

After a moment of what seemed like dead silence, Kerry spoke up, "No one has ever explained it to me like that before."

"Of course not," replied Scott. "Debt is the American way. But think about this for a minute. After graduating high school, most kids these days are going to college, right?"

"Not all of them, but yes, a lot of kids end up going to college," replied Alex.

"And do most kids these days pay cash for college? Or do they end up getting student loans?"

"I would guess most of them get student loans because tuition costs so much, and it goes up each year," Kerry answered.

"Correct." Scott said, "And of course while they're in college they're offered this little plastic thing called a credit card, right? You see these offers all over campuses telling students 'just sign up for a credit card and we'll even give you this free t-shirt!'"

"Yes, I've seen that. So?" asked Alex, impatiently wanting to understand the point behind all of this.

"Well, what happens after these kids finish college and get their first job in the real world? Assuming they actually *can* find a job, which we all know isn't even a guarantee anymore, what's the first new purchase they're dying to make now that they're finally making some money of their own?"

Kerry jumped in, "I know the first thing I wanted! I really wanted a nice car to drive. I had been driving that old Chevy for so long. It had rust holes in it that I could stick my fist through!" She exclaimed, and the three of them laughed. "I worked hard all through college though, and a lot of my friends already had nice cars. I felt like I'd finally earned the right to drive something nice."

"That's exactly right," Scott responded, "that's a pretty typical answer from your average college graduate out on their own for the first time. But do most college grads go out and buy the car they can afford to pay for with cash? Or do most of them go out and get a loan to buy a more expensive car?"

Kerry jumped right into the discussion again, before Alex could even speak, "I know what *I* did. I went out and got a loan. I didn't have the cash to get anything nicer than what I was already driving. I'll never forget that first car payment either. I was so nervous signing off on those loan papers. Now that I look back, it wasn't that much money, but back then it might as well have been a million dollars a month to me!"

"I did the exact same thing," said Alex. "But I would have never been able to have a car as nice as I had without that loan. At least, not for a really long time."

"I understand, Alex," said Scott. "And you're not alone. You did what most of America does today. But stay with me for a minute. Let's say the typical young person, fresh out of college, meets the man or woman of their dreams and gets married. What's the first really big purchase a married couple makes together – usually the largest purchase of their lives?"

"A nice house," Kerry said, "That's what I wanted. A home where we could start our marriage and eventually, our family.

"Correct again, Kerry. Have you and I had this conversation before? You seem to know all the answers!" Scott laughed, amused at how often he'd heard these same answers. "When a newly married couple buys their first home, do they save up for a number of years before buying the house so that they can pay cash? Or do most of them go out and get a loan instead?"

Alex replied, "Of course, most of them get a loan. Isn't that what we're taught? I mean, who could afford to go out and pay cash for a house, especially a newly married couple? That would take forever."

"I hear you," replied Scott. "And many, many years ago, before loans were so readily available, people didn't even have an option to borrow money to buy a home. This meant people had to save up on their own and pay cash. It may have taken a newly married couple a number of years to buy that first home, true, but they would have bought it with cash and owned it outright. These days, that is obviously not the norm—I get it. It's so easy to get access to a loan today, so very few people are willing to do what it takes to own their own home free and clear. But that doesn't mean it's not possible. Many years ago, newly married couples would live with their parents until they could afford their own home, and once they could, all of the townspeople would come together to help build it. It was more of a community effort and less of an 'every man for himself' approach."

"So, what are we supposed to do, go sell our house and move back in with our parents? Are you really suggesting that we go to that extreme?" asked Alex, looking from Scott to Kerry in disbelief.

"I'm not telling you that you should or shouldn't do anything. Here's all I'm saying; the majority of people feel the most freedom in life when they're young. Then they go out into the 'real world.' They get student loans, a couple of credit cards, a car payment or two and then stack on a house payment on top of all of that." Scott ticked the items off on his fingers. "All of these payments require a portion of your time. When you have debt, you're required to go out and serve the lender month after month with a portion of your most valuable asset, the one asset you can never get back once gone – your time – so that you can make money to make the payments. Remember," Scott said, eyebrows raised, "you've promised the lender anywhere from 25-40% of your working hours for the next thirty years of your life, just for your home, not to mention all of the other payments you've promised. Add in a car payment and you just promised more of your working hours away. Add in a credit card payment, a student loan payment and there goes even more of your working hours. Toss in a couple of 'good debt' business loans and whatever else you have on top of that and before you know it, your life is no longer yours. You've promised away your future to the lender, and you must now serve that lender with the majority of your time, thoughts, emotions and actions each and every day, month after month, year after year." Scott paused to let that sink in before continuing. "The minute you stop serving that lender, you lose your car. Or worse, you lose your house. The bill collectors start calling. The fear of loss haunts you, so you serve and serve and serve hoping that eventually you'll make enough money to make it all better. Hoping that one day you can start back at zero. Isn't this true?" He looked across at Alex and Kerry with a serious expression. "Isn't this how you've been living? Isn't that why you work so hard, Alex? So my question to you is this… and if you've heard nothing else today, please hear this… *How can you possibly live a life of ultimate freedom and prosperity when you've already promised away your entire future to the lender?*"

Alex was speechless, his world flipped upside down. Scott remained silent for a moment and let Alex think through it. The more he tried to fight it, the more he knew Scott was right. His brain searched and searched for a flaw in Scott's approach, and just when he almost gave up, he remembered the idea behind his approach to having passive income.

"But it's smart to get a mortgage and build equity, and my rental properties give me passive income."

"Passive income? Come on now, Alex, I've owned rental properties as well, and there's nothing passive about owning single-family homes. They require a lot of work. It's the IRS that classifies it as passive, but I've never been able to just sit back and collect passively, that's a lie!"

Alex leaned back in exasperation. "You know, Scott, I really wish I didn't have any debt. I'm sure that if I made as much as you do, that I wouldn't have any debt either. But you can pay off all your debt because you have the cash. I just don't make that much."

"Really?" Scott raised an eyebrow. "How do you know that I make a lot of money? You really don't know how much I make, do you? How much I make has nothing to do with whether or not I have debt. If anything, the reason I have what I have is because I don't have debt. I get to keep money when I make it because I don't owe it to anyone. I get to spend what I make on whatever I want because I owe nothing to anyone. It's likely I could live a great life off of just the interest you're paying on your loans each year."

Alex wasn't sure that was the entire reason. "Just because you get to keep it doesn't mean that you don't make a killing," he said sourly.

"If I choose to give my money away, I can—to whomever I want. But, Alex, you have no choice but to give it to your lenders. Do you remember when you got that loan on your home? Remember when they approved your loan with the big red stamp of approval? Do you remember seeing the bolded red letters "APPROVED" on your application? How differently would you have felt if that stamp said "ENSLAVED" instead?"

"I know, I know. 'The borrower is slave to the lender.'" Alex conceded grumpily, his frustration starting to get the better of him.

"You're exactly right. But listen, I'm not trying to chew you out. I know I'm in the minority here. I'm just trying to share the freedom I've found. I'm not asking you to put a 'for sale' sign on your house today or fork over your car keys."

"Well, that's good because that would put me over the edge." Alex tried to force a joke, but he wasn't feeling lighthearted.

"You know, this wasn't easy for me either." Alex looked up at him with a flash of curiosity, and Scott continued. "Trust me, when I first heard the word *Lifeonaire* and the principles, I was pretty spooked. I know what you're wrestling with. Starting out, I had a great job in sales and was really moving up. By the time my son Chris was born, I was a manager, and by the time he went to kindergarten, I told managers what to do. From most people's perspective I had it made..." His voice trailed off for a minute. "But it was just the opposite. I was home for dinner so rarely that Chris was confused when I showed up. Even when I was home, I may have been physically there but I wasn't really there. I'd be engrossed in paperwork and then pass out in front of the TV.

"It took a lot for me to see that it wasn't worth the price I was paying. And it didn't happen overnight, that's for sure. But I finally started to make choices based on goals other than just making money. I won't lie, it was a hard road. It's still hard sometimes. But the rewards have made it more than worth it—and it's far better than selling my soul for a paycheck ever was."

Alex and Kerry sat silently, processing it all. Maybe this guy knew where he was coming from after all.

Scott continued. "I'm not trying to push something on you just because it's what's worked for me. Anyway, that wouldn't work—I can't change your heart, and that's where such a big lifestyle change has to come from. But Alex, you know that what you've been doing isn't working. It couldn't hurt to try another way."

This isn't something you just try, Alex thought. "I guess not."

"I'm not asking for any commitments, just that you'll consider what we've talked about today before dismissing it completely. Fair enough?"

"Fair enough. But what's the answer?" Alex asked, ready to get to the point. "How do Kerry and I get a life? What's the first step? Let's get on with this thing."

Scott looked evenly at him. "We're doing that right now," he said, spreading his hands. "I told you, it's a mind-set thing. It's a heart thing. It's more of a journey than a task list of items to be checked off, and I'm taking you on the same journey I went on."

"Now you're sounding all shaman again on me. If you get too metaphysical you're going to lose me quick. You should be able to tell by now that I'm a pretty down-to-earth kind of guy, not an intellectual fruitake!" Alex smiled, though he was half-serious.

"I'm no intellectual either, although maybe I *am* a bit of a fruitcake." Scott smiled back. "There's a difference between theory and practice, and I'm talking from my personal experiences, not just classroom lectures. Everything I'm telling you is based on what I've been through myself and what I've helped many others to overcome. I've been where you are. I've gone down that road the hard way and I've been given the gift of seeing both sides. I've been a slave and I've been free, so what I share with you is shared from my heart and my real life experience, not just fluff. I'm sure that you could teach me a thing or two about construction that I don't know."

Every time Alex tried to put up a wall, Scott gently set the bricks aside before he could get the mortar in to hold it together. It was impossible to argue with Scott, mostly because Alex couldn't argue with something that made sense without being intellectually dishonest. There was no way around what Scott was saying, and he was starting to come to terms with that.

"All right," Alex said, holding his hands up in mock surrender. "Checkmate. You've got my interest up enough that I want to continue this after I've had some time to think about it." He turned to his wife. "Kerry, you're being awfully quiet over there, and you're supposed to be my partner here, not just an observer."

"I'm still here," Kerry said, looking up from the spot on the table she'd been staring at for several minutes. "I'm just thinking. I agree with Alex, I do want to hear more. I want to know more about what it means to be a Lifeonaire, or whatever view it is on prosperity and freedom. I'm not sure exactly what it is just yet, but something you said struck a chord in me, and I need to figure that out. Alex, when are you meeting with John?"

Alex's face turned red and Kerry quickly realized that she shouldn't have said that. Obviously there was nothing set up yet.

"I…uh…yeah, Scott, I was going to ask you about that today. I have a business deal I'm working that I would like to talk to John about. Do you think you could set up a meeting with him for me? I was going to ask him myself the other day, but then the school thing came up with his kid and…" Alex trailed off, flustered.

"I'll tell you what, Alex," Scott grinned at him, looking as if he knew all along that this was one of Alex's motives in coming. "I'll get you a meeting with John separate from our little lunches here, so you can talk business-business instead of metaphysical business. But only if you agree to meet with me for lunch on Fridays for the next, let's say, six weeks. I'd like to continue these talks too. I'll also give you some other little assignments to do, like the vision sheet that the two of you did last night. Nothing major, just some things to get you thinking and moving in the right direction. Deal?"

Alex's heart sank. He wasn't sure this deal would still be around six weeks from now. But he also realized he didn't have much of a choice in the matter. Alex was in no position to negotiate fewer meetings before getting what he really wanted–the introduction to John, and there was a part of him that realized that another 6 meetings like this would probably be good for him.

Alex and Kerry looked at each other for a second and then Alex looked back at Scott. "Deal. I don't see how a lunch every week can hurt, and you might just teach this tired, old dog some new tricks." Alex was smiling, and the mood was generally good around the table. Kerry was feeling a sense of relief and hope at the same time. She really hoped that this would somehow help their finances and their marriage, but she was also wary enough to not expect a miracle.

"Hey, how well do you know John, anyway?" Alex asked. *Better make sure this will be worth it,* he thought.

"Oh, man, he's like my brother. We're pretty tight, and he's a great guy. He's actually giving a lot, building a community center not too far from your place, near the old elementary school. His eyes light up each time he talks about this place. It's going to have a gym and a couple playgrounds, even a small library and…"

Alex began adding numbers in his head as Scott spoke. *That could be a real money-maker! And if it leads to more work in the future…I've got to get a bid in on that…*

"All in all, he's a great guy. We work on being Lifeonaires together. John will be the first person to tell you that before his Lifeonaire days, his money only helped him to be miserable in nicer places. We get a good chuckle out of that one. Our sons are close to the same age and one of the things we both had to do when becoming Lifeonaires was find fun things we could do with our boys. John and I used to work all the time for many reasons, but one major reason was that we honestly didn't know what we wanted to do with our time off. But nowadays we do a lot of fishing, hiking, we play music together, all kinds of stuff. I'm really looking forward to the campout we're going on with our sons in June."

Campouts? Kerry thought, carefully avoiding glancing at her husband. *I really hope that Alex is hearing Scott right now. Justin needs this time badly. He may be a teenager but he still needs his daddy. Please God, if you're out there, if you care about this family at all, please help Alex see this and make his son a priority like Scott and John are doing.*

Campouts? Fishing? Hiking? Who has time for all of those things? Alex simultaneously wondered. *I'm sure Kerry just picked up on the fact that they're taking their kids camping and now there's going to be a big argument over why I can't do the same. How on earth can they manage to be gone for a week in the woods with a bunch of kids? A week off for camping, Europe for a month… Who does stuff like this? Nevermind. I just need to figure out a way to make that camping trip with Justin. After all, nothing seals a deal like having something in common, and maybe I can break the ice and build some rapport with John by talking about how we both recently went camping with our sons.*

"Okay, before we go, I want to share one more principle with you. You must master money in order to master life. Go ahead, write that down. Master money to master life. That starts with understanding how money really works." Scott hopped up from the booth. "I'll meet you here next Friday, same time. If you need me for anything before then, you've got my cell number. If you can both make it back that's great, but I'll at least expect to see you, Alex. I want the two of you to talk about something between now and then. This question will help you more with developing your vision. If you only had three months left to live, what would you do with your life?"

"Is this like the three things you could take with you if you were trapped on a desert island?" Alex laughed.

Scott smiled back. "Something like that. Give it some serious thought, though, and let me know next week what your plans would be. This will help you get clarity with your vision." He plopped the money for the lunches down on the table and tipped an imaginary hat to Kerry. "Ma'am."

Kerry smiled. "Why thank you, kind sir, and thank you for the lunch," she answered in her best Southern belle accent.

"Maybe I'll see the two of you at church this Sunday?" Scott asked hopefully, not expecting a real answer.

"Um, maybe," answered Alex evasively.

"Okay then." Scott turned and walked toward the door and through it, waving at another table as he did so.

Alex turned to Kerry after Scott had left and said, "Well?"

"Not a typical lunch date, I'll give you that," she said. "I hope something positive comes out of all this."

"Me too," said Alex as they got up to leave.

Chapter

5

Although they had agreed to take a few days to think through the "assignment" from Scott before they started writing it out, both Kerry and Alex ended up working on it within twenty-four hours. They both had ideas running through their brains, and neither of them wanted to forget anything before they had a chance to sit down together. By Monday, they decided that they were ready to share their notes with each other. The weekend had unfortunately not been a relaxing one, as Alex had no fewer than three "emergency" calls from his crew, none of which turned out to be an actual emergency, but all of which took up a great deal of time. They hadn't made it to church on Sunday, but then again, they hadn't really planned to go anyway.

Now they agreed that it was time to take time for themselves.

As they sat at the table organizing their notes, there was some excitement in the air between them. These exercises were good for them—the closest thing they'd had to quality time in years. Maybe it was just the experience of sharing something new together, but whatever the reason, this was something they were both looking forward to. That was reason enough to be excited.

"Okay, before we get into details, tell me how you would sum up your three-month plan." Alex smiled at Kerry, making a small game of it.

"I would say...I guess to summarize it, I would say that my plan would be to enjoy every moment with my family," Kerry replied, smiling back at her husband. "And yours?"

"I really struggled with this. I found myself wanting to focus on financial security for my family, though I knew that wasn't the most important thing. I have such a hard time taking my focus off money, it's so ingrained into the way that I think," Alex said, feeling proud of his lofty goal but somehow ashamed when he compared to Kerry's summary. That was idealism talking, though; in reality, his financial security plan made much more sense than her plan to just spend all their time with the family.

"All right," he continued, "tell me about your last three months on Earth."

"Well, it was more general stuff than specifics," Kerry replied, "but okay. We would spend pretty much all our time together as a family between now and then. Something like Justin's camping trip wouldn't be up for discussion, that's for sure, and I would go on it myself if I thought I could tear myself away from Heather for a weekend." She was excited to talk about what her last three months alive would look like if she had her choice, although it seemed kind of weird. Normally talking about dying would be gloomy, but they weren't really talking about the dying part, were they? *I'm talking about the living part*, she thought. "I guess it's been a dream of mine to have more family time in our life, so if I was going to go that's what would be the most important thing to me, that we actually did it for once."

Her voice went through a range of emotions, going from fun to sad to excited to melancholy. At least that's how it seemed to Alex as he listened, and he felt a little small. After all, he was about to pour numbers out on the table when Kerry had just laid her heart out. It didn't seem fair somehow. "Does that give you enough of an idea?" she asked innocently. "Or did you want more specifics?"

"No, I get it. I think I have a good understanding of what you're thinking about. Mine was similar, but more practical," he said with the slightest sheepishness to his tone. "It was to make sure that you and the kids would be taken care of once I was gone. Financially, I mean. I'd want to spend time with you, but…"

Kerry never once took his plan as anything other than great as she listened to him lay out the numbers and the shifting of accounts around, the legal aspects that would need to be covered. She loved him and she knew who he was and how he worked. This was not unexpected. *Got to love him*, she thought. *He is thorough, and he's trying to show love this way.*

When he had finished with his short business plan for his death, Alex asked her, "So, don't you think that would cover everything?"

Kerry smiled. She knew she would have to do a little teaching herself, and she hoped it didn't come out as fussing. "I think it would absolutely cover everything," she said. "How much time do you think it would take to get that all together? The whole three months?"

Alex answered with enthusiasm at having been asked the question. He was getting to talk about something he liked and was good at after all. He explained that he would be able to get everything done in less than two and a half months, even if he were debilitated toward the end. He showed her how he'd planned it to make sure that everything got handled. "Pretty decent planning, huh?" he grinned at her, pleased with his own strategic prowess.

"That's really thinking ahead," she said, studying him. "Honey, if I throw something out there, will you promise not to take it as a criticism, but just an observation?"

This brought Alex down a notch or two from his numbers high, but he was feeling good enough to play this game without getting upset. At least he thought so. "Sure, I'll put my objective hat on," he said, sitting straight up in his chair like he was coming to attention at a formal gathering. Kerry giggled a little at that.

"Okay, but you have to promise," she reiterated.

"Cross my heart and hope to…well, maybe that's not the best way to say it, in light of our discussion," he smiled. "I promise."

"All right, well what I was thinking while you were telling me your plan, I mean, what would Justin and Heather want of you if you had only three months? Do you think that they would want you to spend all your time getting our finances in order? What would they want if you asked them?"

This was a rhetorical question with an obvious answer. Alex knew that the finances were important, but at her words, he realized that they weren't the most important thing, and that he had his priorities in the wrong order. He knew that spending time with his family was important but was also a challenge for him. Making money and dealing with finances sort of came naturally so working this plan had been effortless to him. Spending time with the family would be more work. By default, therefore, he would pursue finances over relationships. He tried to convince himself that he was right because it was easy.

"Well, the thought ran through my mind that if you could plan all that out with so little time, why couldn't you plan out more things with us while you were still here?" Kerry continued tentatively. "It sure would be awesome to feel like you wanted to spend time with the kids and me with that kind of urgency."

Alex got defensive for a second but worked to control that feeling and put it aside to study the question objectively. He wasn't proud of what he saw from that angle.

"You're absolutely right," he said, "but I don't even know how to adjust things to make that possible in our present circumstances." He was looking at her, hoping she had an answer to that particular quandary, which of course she didn't. What she did have was the best follow-up he'd heard in a while.

"I don't either. The question isn't if you know, though, but if you're willing to figure it out." She looked at him lovingly, almost pleadingly, without any hint of accusation or anger. She definitely wasn't trying to fight.

"Of course I am, don't you think I want the same thing?" he asked, almost incredulously. He couldn't imagine that she really thought he didn't care about her or the kids.

"No, I think you do, I just think you just have to figure some things out internally. I don't think you really know that to be true," she said softly. "Like Justin's campout. If it were really important to spend time with him, you'd make it work, just like you did in your plan. Do you see what I'm saying?"

He sat and thought about that. Not about whether she was right; she was definitely right, and he knew it. He was thinking about why he'd never thought about that before and what he could do about it. In that moment, things changed, and everything became more clear.

• • •

As reluctant as he was to admit it, Alex was beginning to look forward to Fridays. Scott was, admittedly, more than a little strange; but it was a kind of strange that Alex was starting to think he might want—at least a little. He pulled into the Cup of Hope parking lot just before noon and walked in to see Scott already chatting it up with two guys behind the counter.

He paused by the door and watched Scott as he appeared to absorb what the two young men were saying. It came as no surprise to Alex that they seemed to enjoy chatting with their familiar customer. Scott seemed to listen with something more than just his ears.

Alex lingered for a moment then reached behind him and pushed the door open and allowed it to close again with a jingle. Scott turned at the sound and gave him a quick wave. "Missed you on Sunday! Grab a table—I'll be there in a minute."

Scott turned back to the counter and Alex settled into his now-usual spot. Scott slid in across from him about five minutes later with two coffees in hand. "Great guys. I love how full of life they are... So where were we?"

"Giving me three months to live."

Scott chuckled. "And...?"

Alex sucked in a breath. "I'd make sure that my family was taken care of. I crunched all the numbers and realized I could actually do that in less than three months, even if I were partially debilitated."

"And how did that make you feel?"

"Whoa! Since when are you a shrink?" Alex ribbed. *At least he made it easy for me to bring up Kerry's request.* "Next thing I know, you'll be asking me to tell you about my childhood."

Scott smiled, shaking his head. "Actually, that's not a bad place to start when we're talking about attitudes about money, but we can save that discussion for another time."

"Anyway, I was feeling all proud of myself for coming up with such a great plan, when Kerry observed that if I could find time to fit in all that in just three months, why couldn't I find more time to do things with my family while I'm still around."

"It's a good question."

"Yeah," admitted Alex, fumbling with his coffee stirrer distractedly. "But it's one I don't have an answer for. Kerry asked me to try to figure out how to spend more time with her and the kids, but I have no idea where to start. And I'm a little afraid to find out."

"So what did you tell her?" Scott asked carefully.

Alex stared into his cup for a moment before replying. "That I'd try. The truth is, I'm not even sure how to do that. I have so many demands on my time right now that I can't imagine taking it easy. I know I need to spend more time going camping with Justin or taking Heather out and showing her how a lady should be treated. And I want to. I want to take Kerry on more dates and have the time to linger with her over a cup of coffee on a Saturday morning. I didn't even know that I wanted to, but now I realize that I do. I just don't see how I can."

Scott just looked at him with a probing, knowing eye, and Alex continued, "I'm stuck. I'm not the father or the husband that I want to be, but how can I be? I can't sacrifice providing for my family to spend time with them! We'd be spending time on the streets!" He was surprised to feel the tiniest lump rising in his throat. *Pull it together, man.*

Scott smiled, but his eyes were sober. "I know that feeling well."

Alex fought the urge to argue. *Yeah, right. You've got it all together.*

Scott nodded. "I know, I know—it's not quite the impression I've given you so far. But believe me, I know where you're coming from. It's why I'm so passionate about sharing what I've learned with others—because I've been on both sides. I remember spending an entire school play in the parking lot because I was on the phone! I missed out on a lot of opportunities to invest in my family. But I can tell you for certain that there's another way, no matter how stuck you think you are."

Both men were silent for a few moments, then Alex spoke up. "I had no idea. I figured you always had it figured out."

That made Scott laugh, harder than he had all day. "Far from it."

"So how did you do it?"

"It all comes down to choices. I couldn't just realize that I wanted to spend more time with the people that mattered most and leave it at that. I had to choose, day after day, to invest in them rather than in earning money. It requires intentionally breaking the patterns we so easily fall into."

Alex let that sink in. "I get what you're saying, but I'm still lost about how to do it."

"We'll get there," Scott reassured him. "For now, let me ask you something."

For once, Alex was happy to be asked another soul-searching question. He nodded.

"If a stranger were to observe your life for a week, taking note of how you spend your time, what would they say is most important to you?"

Alex opened his mouth, but Scott stopped him. "I'm not asking you to answer that now, just to think about it. And after you think about it, ask yourself what you think your kids see. How would they rank your priorities?"

"But my kids are the whole reason that I work so much! I want them to have all they need."

Scott raised an eyebrow. "Really? Did they have any say in that? What do you think they would say if you asked them whether they'd like you to make more money or spend more time with them?"

Alex laughed. "Kerry asked me a very similar question, but they don't understand. If I could just make a little more money, things would be better. They don't understand that yet, especially Heather. They don't know what it's like to worry about money."

"If you don't mind me asking, how much more do you need to make every year?"

"Well, another $30,000 or $40,000 would make all the difference."

"So just 'a little bit more'?"

Alex nodded. "Yeah, that's really all we would need—not much more, but more than we're making now."

"How long ago was it that you and Kerry were living on just $30,000 or $40,000 a year?"

"Well, I was probably twenty-three or so. It was longer ago than I'd like to admit, but I suppose it wasn't actually that long ago."

"And how was life then?"

"A lot simpler, but that was then."

"Tell me what your weeks looked like then."

"Well, we usually spent Saturdays at the park and evenings hanging out on the balcony of our apartment. We didn't have a lot, but we had fun with each other. We didn't really worry about money because we didn't have many responsibilities. Now that I think about it, things were pretty easy. We didn't know how easy we had it! We dreamed of having more. Now we have more stuff, but we don't have the freedom we had then."

Alex took a big swig of the now-lukewarm coffee and realized that he was sort of condemning himself with that statement. Suddenly his self-defense mode kicked in. *He can't be suggesting that we go back to that!* he thought. *Yeah, life was easy then, but we have responsibilities and kids now. We have bills to pay! So he wants me to just stop trying to make enough to pay them? Is he saying my business is bad for my family? My family is the whole reason I started this business! He's crazy and everyone else would think I'm crazy if I follow his plan.*

Scott interrupted his thoughts. "So why can't your life be simpler again?"

Alex raised his eyebrows. "You seriously have to ask that? I can't just go back. I can't just let go of my responsibilities. You're the one who said that I need to choose my family, and ignoring my responsibilities would be disastrous for them. My family is the reason that I want to talk to John about that deal. It's a new beachfront property, and if I can get the funds together, we'd be set, financially."

All at once, Alex switched gears and realized that he had an opportunity here. He'd never taken the "freedom file" out of his briefcase, and it might be the very thing he needed right now. *If Scott has his finances figured out, why shouldn't I ask him to go in on this as well as John?* He pulled it out and spread the papers out in front of him.

Scott looked down obligingly. "So this is down on the coast? That's what—three or four hours away?" he asked.

"About four. If I can pull this off, I'd stay there for the week and come home on the weekends during the project."

"I see… Alex, why do you want this?"

Alex made a face. "What kind of question is that? My life would be better. Things would be better for my whole family! We'd make enough money that we'd never have to worry again. You'd never have to worry again, either, if you go in on this with me. I'd love for you to have a piece of this, too!" Alex could hear himself pitching the idea, and something about it seemed off, like he'd suddenly become the shallow person he was trying to move away from, but he put that thought to the side.

"What would this do for me, exactly?"

Alex fought an eye roll. "Well, for starters, you could make a whole lot more." He leaned in and whispered, "You could go anywhere you wanted for lunch." Scott laughed but let him continue. "And you could invest in a cabin in the woods or take your family wherever they'd like to go on vacation. You could retire early, maybe in less than ten years!"

"And then what?"

"And then, whatever you wanted! You could spend time with your family, actually do things with your friends and relax with your wife. You could do stuff at church and not have to worry about getting to work. Don't you want that?"

Scott was silent for a moment then looked Alex in the eyes. "But I already have all that. You have those things waiting in the wings, especially your family. Speaking of which, I really enjoyed having Justin around last week. You mentioned that he had to be picked up from school—did he have a better week this week?

Alex sighed. This wasn't what he wanted to talk about, but he had to keep Scott on his team. "I don't know. He got sent home last week because they caught him smoking. I have no idea where he got the idea that that's okay. Kerry says that he's been hanging around with the wrong crowd, but I'm not sure what I can do about it. I can't just get rid of his friends. I mean, he sees these guys at school every day."

"Justin has a lot of factors in his life that are influencing him, doesn't he?"

"He does," Alex agreed, "but he should know better. We've always taught him what's right. It's like he's purposely ignoring the two people in his life who care about him most. He's important to us—both our kids are—but he just doesn't get it. Those guys he's hanging around don't care about him, but he seems to care a lot about what they think. I do all I do for him and for Heather. I want what's best for him—it's not like I told him not to smoke so that I could punish him! I care and he just ignores me!"

"That sounds familiar," mused Scott. "Every time I feel that way about Chris, or someone who works for me, I can't help but wonder how often God feels that way about me and my actions. He has a plan for us, one that's for our own good, but we ignore it for what's more enticing in the short run."

"Well, I don't see how his behavior is enticing. The guys he's been hanging out with aren't even that nice to him. But I guess I'm not much competition. I heard what he said to you last week—how adamantly he said he didn't want to do what I do for a living when he grows up. I mean, I wasn't sure if he would follow in my footsteps, but I thought he at least respected what I did. If he doesn't want to go into real estate or construction, fine, but he's on the road to screwing up his life."

"Alex, what do you want your son's life to look like when he grows up?"

C'mon Scott... are you going to do this deal with me or not? "I just want him to be happy and successful—to have a career that gives him security, maybe a wife and kids. But that's not going to happen if he doesn't shape up. He's going to be a screwup, and I have no idea how to stop him."

"Remember what you said to me last week when we were playing LIFE? About how you didn't know anyone who's living your idea of a prosperous life?"

"Uh, I think so." Alex wasn't sure what this had to do with Justin, but he played along.

"Well, you had a good point. Most people live their lives like they play that game, trying to reach certain milestones to become more successful. But what if that wasn't the goal of the game? What if the winner was the person who had the best life experiences? Or, in my case, the person who brought the most glory to God? Would life look any different?"

"It would change your strategy, I guess."

"Exactly. So would you make different decisions then?"

"I guess so. I'd take Kerry out more and plan fun things on the weekends. I'd put Heather in bed every night because I really do love that cuddle time with her. I'd probably even make the kids breakfast every day before heading out to work." Alex paused. "I'd see my brothers a lot more often too. I hardly see them anymore."

"Do you ever do *any* of that now?"

"Rarely. I don't have time."

"Let me ask you something: what do you do when you know an important client wants to meet with you in the coming week? Do you say, 'Sure, I hope it works out'? Or do you plan a time that works for both of you?"

"I plan it, of course," Alex replied, reluctantly starting to see a connection.

"Why?"

"Because if I don't, it probably wouldn't happen. I'm a busy guy."

"Right. Just about everything in life is like that. If we don't plan what's important, it won't happen. Time passes, and Life goes on without us because we're too busy pursuing money and our ideas of success. This becomes our default setting because we don't know what else to pursue. And our default settings influence those around us."

Alex breathed out slowly. "Like Justin."

"*Especially* Justin. He watches you, you know."

"He ignores me," Alex corrected him.

"Not as much as you think. Did you notice how he played LIFE? It was pretty revealing. He was aggressive…he chose the career that would bring him the most money… I think you know where he gets that from."

"Are you sure you're not a shrink? Isn't this what they call 'play therapy' or something like that? I think Justin's a little old for that."

Scott laughed and shook his head. "I'm sure. Just calling it as I see it."

"Well, to be honest, now that you mention it, I see it too. I do influence him. He does what he sees me do, even if he doesn't do what I tell him to…" Alex was interrupted by his buzzing cell phone. After a quick peak, he saw it was Carol, his assistant. "Excuse me," he mumbled to Scott, turning away and answering. He talked for a few moments and then turned back to Scott. "Hey, I've got to get back to work—one of my foremen is having some issues with the township." He slid out of the booth and grabbed his briefcase.

"Okay, but remember this. You have to teach Justin how to live. If you want Justin to live a full life, and he's watching you, you need to be the one who demonstrates how to do it for him. Otherwise, he'll end up just like you."

"Is my life that bad?" asked Alex. "But I get it. I'm not really happy and he's going to end up the same way if this is what I teach him."

"You're right. Well, tell Justin I said hi—Kerry, too. Sorry she couldn't make it today."

"Yeah, me too. Wish she could have heard this. I have a feeling she'd agree with everything you're saying... *again*."

. . .

The kids had already gone to bed, and Alex and Kerry sat across one another at the kitchen table. It wasn't the conversation Alex had expected to have that night with his wife. Sure, he'd told her Scott's seeming disinterest in the beachfront property. But once he mentioned what Scott had said about Justin, there was no changing the subject.

"So Scott told you that you're the one Justin imitates? Just last week you vented about how he always ignores you."

"I know," conceded Alex, "and he does ignore what I say. But he imitates what I do, even if he doesn't like it."

"The same way Heather copies me...and with her only being three, just imagine how much more she's going to copy me as she gets older." Kerry instantly flashed back to earlier that day when she saw Heather rubbing her lips together like she did after applying lipstick. "And what, you're just supposed to choose to spend time with him?" she asked.

"In a nutshell, yes," Alex said, looking for a way to put words to his thoughts. "Scott asked me what I would do differently if the end goal of the game—of life—wasn't to make the most money, but to have the best experiences."

"Okay..."

"And I told him a bunch of stuff: that I'd take you out more, that I'd go visit my brothers and take the kids to see their cousins...and that I'd go on Justin's camping trip."

Kerry's smile wavered a little on that last item. Those other things were great, but... "But I thought you couldn't take a week off from work for that."

"I could if my goals were different. I'd just have to plan for it." He shared what he and Scott had discussed about defaulting to earning money if he didn't plan to do other things and saw a tiny flash of understanding in his wife.

"It's like my spinning classes," she said with a new hint of insight. "I know they're good for me, but if I don't schedule them, there's no way I'll show up. Other things come up, and no matter how good my intentions are, working out gets pushed aside. So, what are we supposed to plan?" She pulled her phone off its charger and opened up the following week's calendar. Alex followed suit. They stared at their own screens then glanced at each other.

"And when exactly?" mumbled Alex. This was going to be interesting...

• • •

On Thursday at rush hour, Alex picked up the phone and hit the speed dial to call Kerry. "Hey, I'm going to be home a little late tonight—I have to check on that renovation property over on Elm Street. Hopefully, it won't take long, but I'll have to fight traffic on the way back."

He heard Kerry sigh. "All right. Try not to be too long. See you in a bit."

He slipped his phone back in his pocket, turned the corner onto Elm, and looked for a parking spot. That's when he looked up at the house and noticed that the door was open. "You idiots left the place wide open!" he shouted to the dashboard since his construction guys had left at least an hour earlier. "You'll be hearing from me tomorrow, and it's not going to be pleasant." He pulled over in front of the house and rushed over to see what else his guys had failed to do.

When he stepped through the doorway, he saw a man with his arms reaching through a hole in the kitchen wall—not one of his guys. Alex paused in confusion then turned bright red as he realized that this guy was cutting the copper pipes to steal them.

"Hey!" he shouted, running toward the thief who promptly dropped his tools and ran for the back door. Alex gained on him as he fiddled with the lock, shouting as he sprinted and leapt over rolls of carpet...then falling hard and suddenly to the floor as he was struck from behind. Pain seared through the back of his head, and though the room was spinning, he made out two sets of hands coming at him with pipes. Even in his disoriented state, he had the good sense to cover his head as the kicks and strikes began.

Time seemed to slow, and with each blow, he saw a scene flash before his eyes...Kerry in her wedding dress...Justin as a baby... Heather's first birthday...

why couldn't he remember more times after his kids got older? He knew why. But why hadn't he done anything to change it? The waterfront property didn't matter. Meeting John didn't matter. Why didn't he see that before? Why?

He began to fade then, and the pain started to feel very far away. He began to go limp.

Vaguely, he heard the men leave and the house went silent. Alex lay still, barely able to breathe, certainly not able to call for help. Minutes passed—or maybe they were hours. His body felt like it had been set on fire, and his clothing stuck to him in a mess of blood and sweat. Finally, gritting his teeth in pain, he slowly reached into his jacket pocket and pulled out his phone. He let it drop by his cheek and hit the speed dial to call Kerry.

Two rings, three.

"Hello?"

"Kerry…" Alex rasped.

"Alex! What's going on? You sound awful! Are you all right?"

"I…I'm not sure. I…I…" Just getting one word out took every ounce of strength he had. "Help." His voice was barely a whisper, but it seemed like a shout in his pounding head.

Kerry's voice rose at least an octave. "Alex! Where are you?"

"Elm Street," he gasped. "Thirteen…fifty-two."

"Okay, Alex, *don't move*. I'm calling 911 and having them send an ambulance! I'll meet you there."

Alex tried to groan out a thank-you, but nothing came out.

"Hang on! I love you!" Kerry hung up, threw on the first pair of shoes she could find, and dialed 911 as she ran to her car.

• • •

Alex opened his eyes and blinked several times as the room—where was he?—came into focus. Kerry's voice cut through the fog.

"Hey, welcome back."

Alex found her voice to his left. "How...where am I?"

"You're at Riverfront Memorial, honey. Do you remember what happened?"

Alex thought. He had gone to check on the Elm Street house. There were men...then it slowly trickled into his brain. "The guy hit me so hard. I didn't even see it coming." His brain continued to sift through the incident, the flashbacks coming slowly...

He tried to sit up but was met with a jabbing pain in his side. Kerry's grip on his hand tightened.

"Easy there. You have a cracked rib...among other things."

Alex winced and tried to relax into his pillow. "What other things?"

"Well, it looks like you were hit in the head pretty hard. You have ten stitches and a concussion...but you're going to be okay." She smiled tearfully at him.

Alex groaned.

"You'll need to take it easy for a while, though."

He groaned again, and the world faded back into sleep.

. . .

Wincing, Alex carefully clicked the passenger's-side seatbelt into place. He had protested the night before when the ER doctor had forbidden him to drive for two weeks, but now he fully understood why. Not only was the sun a little brighter to his eyes than normal, he was also careful not to move too fast so as to avoid the cracked rib digging into his side any more than necessary. When Kerry drove Alex home the night before, he got into the car just a little bit too fast and found himself near tears. He wasn't about to make that same mistake again today.

Kerry turned to him from the driver's seat. "You okay? Are you sure you even want to do this today? No one would blame you if you cancelled."

"Yeah, I'm fine." It was far from convincing, but he wasn't going to miss meeting Scott this week. Not after something finally clicked. Or broke—he wasn't sure which. "Thanks for being willing to call off work to drive me over."

The truth is, Alex couldn't think of anything else but to meet with Scott. He kept rolling the movie reel over and over in his head. *What if yesterday would have been my last day on earth? What if I would have never woken up? Would I ever really care much about half the stuff I do on a daily basis?*

"You're worth it." Kerry smiled as she pulled out of the driveway.

Mercifully, the drive was short, although Alex noticed every single bump in the road, something he would have never paid much attention to just a day ago. He eased himself out of Kerry's SUV and then leaned on the hood to rest for a moment as Kerry came around to take his arm. They had only taken a few steps when Scott came jogging out to meet them.

"Alex! What happened?"

"Rough night the other night." Alex briefly recounted the details of the attack and his injuries.

"Wow. I'm glad you're here, but you could have canceled, you know." Scott said, as taking notice of the bandages wrapped around the back of Alex's head.

"I know—that's what Kerry said. But I wasn't going to miss this." Alex tried to sound better than he felt.

Scott smiled. "Well, I'm flattered. Let's get you inside and sitting somewhere comfortable."

"I'm not sure 'comfortable' exists right now, but that sounds good." Alex said, trying to make a joke out of the situation.

"Ok, then we'll find you a really uncomfortable spot instead," Scott joked.

"Ughh... don't make me laugh!" Alex responded, as he laughed and doubled over in pain at the same time.

They slowly made their way inside and settled into the couch where Alex and Justin had sat to play LIFE. "You want your usual?" Scott asked Alex. "I'm not letting you do anything today."

"Sure. Thanks."

Scott turned to Kerry. "What can I get you?"

"Skim latte, please. Thanks."

"Sure thing. Be right back."

Alex fidgeted, wincing and obviously hurting with each small movement. Kerry grabbed his hand and their eyes met. They didn't need to say anything. They both realized how close they'd come to losing each other, and that they needed to make changes soon. There was no more time to waste. They wanted to start enjoying their lives right now. This very second. Yesterday, if that was possible.

Scott returned, drinks in hand, and settled into a chair across from them. "Looks like you have something to say," he noted, reading the expression on Alex's face.

"You've got that right. Last night, I was doing what I always do; I simply stopped to check on one of my renovations. And I was attacked. This is going to sound really hokey, but I actually saw my life flash before my eyes." Alex paused as if coming to grips for the first time that perhaps he'd been doing it all wrong this whole time. "And I realized that the farther along in my life I got, the fewer memories I had with my family. All of a sudden, I didn't care about closing deals or retiring or any of that. Everything I've been striving for no longer mattered. I just wished for more memories with Kerry, Justin, and Heather. I think I finally get what you've been saying—or at least I get it a lot more than I did."

Scott was beaming. "And what, exactly, do you get?"

"Well, for starters, I get that no amount of providing for my family can replace time with my family. I realized that I really do want to be a better husband and father, enough to do whatever it takes. I don't want my life to end wishing I had spent more time with my family. That's what went through my mind last night." Alex shifted uncomfortably on the couch as he fumbled for words. "I want to be happy...to have time to spend with the people who matter most to me. And don't get me wrong, I want to provide for them too, but not at the expense of everything else."

Kerry nodded in agreement and added, "Yes, spend time together, without always being cut off by some pressing obligations."

"So you may not have all of that time yet, but just for fun let's assume for a moment that you had all the time in the world to do whatever you wanted with your family and life. What would you do with that time?" Scott pressed. When they paused, he grabbed a pen out of his pocket and pushed a notebook in their direction. "Let's make a list. What do you want your life to look like?"

"Well, that month at the beach with no schedule would be nice," suggested Kerry.

"Great—write it down. What else?"

"Time with our kids. Real time—not just time in between the picking them up and running out the door."

"What would that look like?" Scott pressed

"I'd go on that camping trip with Justin," Alex suggested. "And I would be the one to read books to Heather and rock her to sleep every night."

Kerry was starting to catch on as well. "And I'd have more time to spend with Heather too. Maybe I'd work less."

Alex added, "Maybe not at all." Kerry looked at him with big eyes and he smiled. "I'm serious, Kerry. I don't know how to pull something like this off yet, but I think if we really sat down and thought it through and made it important to us, perhaps we could make it work." Kerry added it to the list, more deliberately than she had the other items.

"What else?"

With Scott's help, they continued to brainstorm, slowly filling both sides of the paper. Family dinners… evenings at home…weekend trips to see relatives… rebuilding that old car with Justin, everything that was so simple yet so difficult to make time for before.

When they began to slow down, Scott reached for the list and surveyed it. Now this was what he was looking for. "Well, this is quite a life."

Alex reached for Kerry's hand, and they smiled at one another, not quite sure what to say and almost afraid to hope that the things they'd just committed to paper could become reality.

Scott handed the notebook back to Kerry. "So now comes the real question. How badly do you want this life?"

Alex squeezed Kerry's hand. "More than anything." Kerry nodded and squeezed back. "But how do we get there?"

"Well, you already told me how much you make, Alex," said Scott. "Kerry, would you mind telling me how much you make?"

"About $75,000 a year."

"And what do you do?"

"I work in the marketing department for Jackson Products." She smiled sheepishly. "I always saw myself working to promote something exciting, but it turns out that marketing paper products is a lot more practical."

"Let me ask you something, Kerry. Why do you work?"

"It's not like I have a choice. I have to."

"But didn't you choose your lifestyle?" Scott asked gently. "You could choose to live a very simple life, one that required less income."

Kerry was silent, but it was obvious from her expression that she couldn't argue.

Scott continued. "You've chosen a complicated life, one facet at a time, and all of these things take your time and energy away from the things you really want. You force yourself away from your true desires in favor of maintaining your lifestyle, which, let me remind you, is full of things you don't even currently have time to enjoy."

"But we're in it now," Kerry protested, albeit kindly. "We can't just stop paying for things and live in a tent."

"No, you can't. You didn't get into this lifestyle overnight, and you can't change it overnight. But you can start making choices that lead to a simpler life. Choices that will bring you closer and closer to this list of things we just came up right now rather than waiting until someday later down the road."

"Like what?" asked Alex.

"Well, that truck you're driving is no run-of-the-mill Ford, and I believe that's Kerry's Mercedes SUV in the parking lot, right?"

"That's right. My truck is a King Cab dually F-350, but I use it for work."

"Well, what would happen if you sold the F-350 and the Mercedes and bought a pair of inexpensive used vehicles?"

"Our neighbors would think we'd lost our minds!" exclaimed Kerry.

"So would my colleagues," added Alex. "Anyway, we bought the Mercedes SUV because it was the safest one in its class. It wasn't all about the emblem on the front, you know."

"Okay, but what if you kept your cars as long as they worked rather than automatically getting newer models every couple years?"

Both Alex and Kerry cringed.

"Wouldn't you have more money for other things?"

"Well, yes, but…" Alex hesitated. *We can't do that* *That isn't a good reason,* he thought. *Think of a good reason!*

While Alex trailed off, Scott continued. "And what about your house? Do you really need all that space? What if you moved to a smaller place? I'm not talking a one-room shack, but maybe a couple fewer bedrooms or less property. How would that affect you?"

"I'd have less to clean!" Kerry blurted out, laughing. "But what would everyone think?"

"Yeah, people just don't do that sort of thing willingly," added Alex.

"But you'd have fewer expenses, wouldn't you?"

"Yes." Couldn't argue that one.

"And you'd probably be able to work less because you wouldn't need as much money."

"Probably, but everyone would think we were nuts, or worse yet, that we'd failed!" Alex exclaimed.

"Maybe so," conceded Scott. "But they're all so worried about trying to impress others with their own lives that they really don't care about yours. And why should others determine what you go after in life? Are you living for them or for you?"

Neither Alex or Kerry answered.

"Correct me if I'm wrong, but aren't you allowing your life goals to be written by those around you? If everyone else started moving into smaller homes, you wouldn't have very many qualms about it, would you?"

"No, probably not," Alex admitted softly. Pieces were beginning to click, and he was starting to see his way forward.

"So why not choose your own path and make your own rules to get the life you want?"

Alex scrambled to pull cohesive thoughts together. "I get what you're saying—it actually makes a lot of sense. It probably makes sense to a lot of people, but how many of us do it? I mean, it's not like it's complicated, but it's really hard."

"Do you remember that dollar bill? All that it represents?"

They both nodded, but it was Alex who spoke up. "It's something we work hard for, trading our lives for, but it masters us and doesn't give life back."

"Exactly. Yet in this country we're so focused on money and our lives revolve around getting more at any cost. We define success as a bigger bank account, but we can never get there, because 'bigger' always means 'just a little more.' So we're always slaves to money. Instead of creating a fuller life, we trade away our lives in pursuit of hopefully getting life back someday. Money is the master of the vast majority of Americans, and because of that, very few of us live abundant lives."

Kerry spoke up. "I guess you're right. No matter what I want, I always find something bigger and better to go after once I get it. The things that I've wanted so badly never seem to give the satisfaction that I had hoped."

"You're not alone. Like I said, very few Americans live free, without being mastered by money. The question is, how can you be one of the few who make yourselves free to experience life abundantly?"

"But…but we don't see how we can have that life. It seems idealistic. We don't see how we can afford it and still have time to live it."

Scott could see the turning wheels under the surface of Alex's words. "I think you hit on a really important point, and you're ready for the next principle," he said after a pause. "Alex, do you remember what I said about pursuing money as the default for most Americans?" Alex nodded and Scott continued. "When we fall into that pattern, we trade our lives away for money. It's hard to really live when our lifestyles demand that we trade all our time to feed them."

"You've got that right. But it's not like I can stop paying the bills."

"No, but you can change the rules of the game that you play by. It starts with you. You have to stop promising your future time away to the lender. If you keep playing by the same rules as everyone else, you're going to get the same *results* as everyone else. You've already told me that you don't know anyone who's living the life that you would like to live according to your definition of freedom and prosperity. So I highly recommend that you do something different and make up new rules. Rules where the winner of the game has the best life experiences. But to do this, you need to protect your time."

"It's freedom to live your life on the terms that you desire, not money—that's only a vehicle for living life. Many people have earned a lot of money, but have no freedom, and that's not what they'd hoped for. Once you understand this, everything changes. Your new rules will become the guide that helps you make all the decisions in your life. Not how much you owe or what the lender demands of you," Scott explained. "Right now, instead of making decisions about your life based on what you want, your debt is making those decisions for you. It controls you."

"Said that way, it sounds so simple..." Alex mulled. "But how can I live without debt? Who can buy a house without a mortgage? You have a mortgage, right?"

"Actually, no."

Alex raised his eyebrows. *Wow. This guy is better off than I thought. Well, good for him!* "Well, I'm glad you make enough money that you don't need a mortgage," he snipped. His words came out with more bite than intended. "Sorry, man. It's just... I had no idea. Good for you, though."

"No problem, but you're making a pretty big assumption. What I'm going to share with you is simple. It's just not always easy, and it certainly challenges conventional thinking," Scott countered. "The life I've chosen to live goes against the grain, but it's worth it. And it doesn't mean you have to give up everything in your life either. It just means I started to value the aspects of my vision more than all of the *'things'* that were keeping me from living life right now. I wanted to stop living a complicated life and get down to the basics again of what really made life worth living. The way I figured it, I wanted what was on this list more than anything. Some people looked at it as though I was making sacrifices, but I didn't see it that way at all. I looked at it like I was buying my life back," Scott explained. "Anyway, what's a lot of money to you?"

"That depends," Alex hedged.

"On?"

"On a lot of things…on how much you need, on how much you already have, and on what you want to do with it," Alex replied. "It also depends on how old you are. Heather still gets excited over a nickel, while it takes at least $20 to get a reaction from Justin. It's been a long time since I was thrilled by that much." Alex paused. It felt like a lifetime since he'd gotten excited about a mere $20, but he could remember when it had made his day to hold a bill that large.

"So you'd agree that 'a lot of money' is subjective?"

"Well, sure. If it weren't, I'd have to give the kids a much larger allowance," Alex chuckled, and immediately realized he'd better not crack too many jokes unless the rest of the coffee shop wanted to witness a grown man cry. He carefully took a breath before continuing. "But it's like what we talked about before, when you asked me how long ago Kerry and I had lived on just $30,000 or $40,000 a year. It might not have been 'a lot of money,' but at the time, it was enough. I wouldn't exactly call it enough now." Alex's new eyes were finally starting to serve him well.

Scott smiled, like a parent watching their kid make their first basket or catch their first fly ball. "Well said." He looked Alex in the eye. "So what would you call enough now?"

"I'm not sure anymore. I don't think it's $40,000, but other than that, I have no idea." Alex wasn't sure how small an amount he was ready to consider, when he was talking about 'enough.'

"Well, a lot of that depends on your goal. It's like when I asked how your life would change if the object of the game wasn't to make money but to have the best experiences."

"It would change a lot—I already told you that I'd spend more time with my family. But I was lost on how to do that before, and I'm still lost now. How do you make it work?" Alex asked.

Scott grinned as if he'd been waiting to be asked just this question. "Well, for starters, I don't need much. And since I don't owe anything to anyone, I get to keep what I make. It's not about making a lot, but about having the freedom to do whatever I choose with what I make." He watched Alex's face, hoping that it would click.

Something *did* click. Alex began doing a bit of quick math in his head. *If he makes even a quarter of what I do but gets to keep it, he's living a pretty sweet life. But if he makes as much as I do, there's hardly a limit to how he could live...*

Scott seemed to read his mind. "Remember, the goal isn't the money. It's to have the best experiences and, in my case, to live in a way that pleases God. How you use money to reach your goal is what matters, not how much money you have. No matter how much or how little you have, it's what you do with it that counts, and your rules will determine that. And setting the rules, basically setting yourself up to win before you start making decisions is the best way to make sure that the choices you make help you get closer to what you really want in life."

"I think we're a little past that," Alex replied. "You know how old we are—I would have had to have figured out my goals over twenty years ago!"

"Hey, I didn't do it when I was younger, either. And, like you, I fell into the default mode of earning money and pursuing as much as I could, thinking that was the ticket to life. But when we allow our culture to write the rules of abundant living, we become stuck serving those types of lifestyles. And as you know, that lifestyle doesn't give us what we want—the *time* to experience abundant lives."

"I feel like I haven't had time for anything other than work for years," Alex admitted, glancing at Kerry sheepishly. "And I think I'm finally starting to understand why."

"Enlighten me," Scott said, grinning.

"Well, I think it's because we just jumped in. I threw myself into a job where I could make a lot of money because it seemed like the best thing to do at the time, but I never really thought about how it would affect my life decades down the road." He looked at Scott. "I think I'm getting this right?"

"You're spot on. You didn't make a plan, so you followed the plan that was preached by the world around you. And the plan that the world preaches is a complicated one. It tells you that you need to trade away your life so that you can one day *experience* life. And we fall for it."

Alex breathed a sigh of relief. "Finally, I'm starting to get it...*starting* to. But it seems difficult to change things now."

"Actually, experiencing prosperity is simple, but most of us complicate life by playing a game that's difficult—probably impossible—to win. But it doesn't have to be that way! When we follow the right plan in the right order, we can set ourselves up to win the game of life every time. But that can't happen when we let the world's rules complicate the game. It's what Lifeonaire's call prosperity through simplicity. This is the next principle. Write it down."

Alex wrote down *prosperity through simplicity* and pondered that for a moment. "You're making this sound so simple—no pun intended," Alex replied. "But practically speaking, it's not nearly so easy."

"Remember, it's all about perspective. And trust me, I've been on both ends of the spectrum. Sure, I've made a lot of money, but back about 12 years ago I only needed around $24,000 a year to get by. That's all I needed. If I made more than that, I could spend it on whatever I wanted. But life was very simple back then. Three years later, things started to really kick off in my business and I made more than that every two weeks. If I'd kept the lifestyle I had before I started making all the money, I could have worked half of January and been set for the year, but that's not what I did. I found plenty of ways to use my earnings just as fast as they came in. And according to the world, according the books and tapes out there that teach all of the financial principles that supposedly work the best, I was doing everything right. I had lots of business deals going, and with all of that came a lot of fixed overhead. I had a big house, a vacation house on the shore, and more tech toys than I could use. Even my accountant said I was doing everything right and actually encouraged me to go out and buy more toys so I could use the write-offs. On the outside, everyone looked at me as a role model. They all thought I had it made. And it certainly appeared that way. But I didn't feel free. Not one bit. Just 12 years ago, making very little money, I was free. Then fast forward just a few years and the amount of money I needed to make ends meet for an entire year was what I now needed just to get me through two weeks. If I was free 12 years ago making only $24,000 per year, how is it that I wasn't free just a few years later making that much every two weeks? My point is, the more we pursue money, the more we create a need for it, because we cultivate a life that depends on it. And the more money we need, the more of our lives we trade away for it. It's not that there's anything wrong with earning money, but when we give up all our lives for it, then something is very wrong."

Kerry chimed in, nodding her head. "It's all starting to make sense to me now."

"Good, now I want the two of you to dwell on that over the course of the next week. I have to get running now, but the next time we get together, we're going to begin talking about the plan. And Alex, please... do yourself a favor and get some rest this week. You need time to heal. Those head bandages went out of style *years* ago!"

Chapter

6

"Well, when you say it like that, it makes perfect sense…and none at all, all at the same time!" Kerry exclaimed. She and Alex sat next to each other on the swing on the deck. They'd already been there for over an hour. She'd listened to Alex talk all the way home from Cup of Hope and well into the evening about what Scott had said in regard to debt. Although his body was clearly exhausted from all of the activity and injuries, his brain seemed to be working like a well-oiled machine. Alex didn't seem one bit tired, although he should have been. It was as if most of the pieces finally fit together, but he—or she, for that matter—couldn't tell what the picture was supposed to be.

"That's exactly what I thought." Alex replied. "In theory, it makes perfect sense, but it flies in the face of everything we've ever heard. You were with me in those finance classes we took years ago. You heard what they said about good debt and bad debt, right?"

"Yeah, debt is supposed to be good if you invest in things that gain value—like our house," Kerry confirmed. "Or make us money. So is Scott saying that we shouldn't have bought our house?"

"I'm not sure. I always thought the house was a good thing. The same thing with most of our debt. maybe not our cars, but much of the rest is supposedly the good kind."

Kerry agreed again and nodded. "And if we didn't have a mortgage, we'd just be throwing money away on rent each month. How can a mortgage be a bad thing?"

"I don't know. It seems like we're missing something, though. I just don't know what it is."

"It seems like we have to give up a lot, and yet Scott doesn't seem like he's hurting for anything," Kerry observed.

"You're right. Last week, he mentioned giving up our house, our cars…but he's got those things. He doesn't have a mortgage, though, so I'm not sure if that counts," Alex admitted. "So how does denying ourselves all this fit with the abundant life he keeps talking about?"

"I don't know…I just don't know…" Kerry rubbed her temples tiredly. "We want to have 'life' as Scott calls it, but giving up everything…I just don't know," she repeated. "What else can I say? The path to life seems crystal clear and yet completely blocked all at the same time."

Alex was equally torn. "I don't know either. Giving up our lifestyle—getting a smaller house, cheaper cars—seems crazy, torturous even, but I can't shake what Scott said about trying another way. I don't want debt to control us, but are we willing to give up everything so that we can take that new path?"

They both stared out into the night, lost in thought and out of things to say. Finally, Kerry spoke up. "Alex, could I come with you next Friday?"

Alex was taken aback. "Well, sure, but I thought you couldn't take any more time off."

"I can. I probably shouldn't, but I think I need to. I'll just stay late or go in early or something—I'll figure it out. I just think we need to talk to Scott about this together if we're going to figure it out."

· · ·

As always, Friday came quickly, but this week seemed to be full of more sleepless nights and constant wondering what life would be like "if." It was hard enough to sleep with all of these thoughts running through Alex's head, much less the fact that stitches tend to itch like crazy as he was healing. Alex was thankful that he was to the point now where a whole hour would go by before he was reminded of his injuries. Throughout the past week, as he reflected on their discussion from the week prior, he was excited by the glimpses of hope for the future that he was feeling. But there were flashes of fear as well. And this week, Alex was also nervous— the nervousness that came when you were close to the truth and it scared you to death.

They arrived at Cup of Hope, and Kerry pulled into their usual spot; Scott said hello as always, and they settled into "their" table. But something was different. This time, Alex and Kerry came with a goal that both terrified and thrilled them—to figure out what the picture really was and then face the decision to jump on board or run away.

"Good to see you again, Kerry," Scott said as they settled in. "To what do I owe the pleasure?"

Truth time! "Well, from what Alex has told me, you're right. We're stuck. And confused. I mean, you keep talking about actually living life, and we want that, but you also talked about giving up our house and cars. How does living fit in with denying ourselves so much? That doesn't sound like living well." She looked at Scott expectantly.

"It's not easy, especially at first," Scott admitted. "I know that it feels like you're denying yourself, but I'm not asking you to deny yourself of good things. I'm suggesting that you embrace what it is that you really want rather than what society tells you to have. If what you really want is life, then the answer will come much easier to you. The good news is; you get to choose. At first, it may sound like you're giving up a lot, however, the truth is that you're not giving up anything at all. By simplifying and getting out of debt, you're actually getting your life back," he explained. "Right now, you both have a lot of what the world says you should have, but the one thing you don't have, according to your own words, is life. I'm simply asking you what is more important to you, staying in debt and keeping some of the things you currently have? Or simplifying a little bit so that you can have your life back? This is usually the quickest and easiest path to becoming a true Lifeonaire."

"But that's part of what we don't get," Kerry interjected. "We understand the part about how debt controls you, but isn't that better than, say, throwing money away on rent every month without ever having something that's yours to show for it?"

"We were always told that a house was good debt," Alex added.

"Who told you that? What was *their* goal for *your* life? Scott challenged them. "If your goal in life is to make and accumulate as much as you can, then sure, a house is great. But if your goal in life is to be free, like I've said, that changes the rules of the game. Let me ask you two: would you do more with your lives if you didn't have a mortgage?"

Alex and Kerry looked at one another, silently determining who would field the question. Kerry tackled it. "I'm sure we would. I'm not sure what we'd do exactly, but the pressure would be off."

Then Alex chimed in. "We could take time off if we wanted to without worrying how we'd pay the bill. Maybe we wouldn't have such a large payment if we were just paying rent. I know we wouldn't have to pay for house repairs and such." He thought back to his conversation with Kerry and added, "But just because life would be different, does that mean that owning a home is bad?"

"Remember when I asked you who owns your house?" Scott asked.

"I think so. You've asked me a lot, you know," Alex replied.

"Well, then I'll ask you again: who owns your house?"

"I'm guessing I said that I do when you asked me before," Alex admitted. "But I'm not so sure I think that anymore. I've only paid for about a third of it—if that."

Scott smiled. "You're catching on. So if you never made another payment, what would happen?"

Alex remembered this part. "The bank would repossess it. It wouldn't be mine at all."

"Exactly. So who owns your house?"

"You don't need to tell me this time—the bank!" Seen through new eyes, this logic was starting to make a little more sense. Still...

Kerry spoke up now. "But the fact is, we already have a mortgage. It's not like we can just stop making payments!"

Scott smiled again. "Another important point. Whenever you have a debt, that debt limits your freedom. In the case of your mortgage, you're not free to stop making payments unless you want to lose your home."

"And that's not an option, so we really don't have a choice but to keep making payments," Kerry added, realization dawning as she spoke. "So maybe a mortgage is good debt compared to, say, running up your credit card, but it still limits us."

"Exactly. It might not give you a bad credit score, but it can still rob you of your freedom," Scott agreed. "You've promised to serve the lender for the next thirty years of your life to pay for the home. Along with taking care of the home, paying taxes on it, decorating it, cleaning it, and other things that come along with home-ownership, you've probably committed more than 50 percent of your working hours for the next thirty years of your life to that. When you get up and go to work on Monday morning, Kerry, it's not because you want to, it's because you *have* to. That's the part that we can't shake. You no longer get to choose what you do. The lender has a say in how you spend your time."

Kerry barely heard him and barely heard the rest of the conversation. She was still pondering that flash of understanding, still looking in wonder at one simple truth that had just come into focus for the first time. *Life was all about freedom… Giving some things up for the sake of freedom meant getting life… Maybe it wasn't deprivation after all…* She continued to spin the thoughts in her mind, tossing them like socks in the dryer in hopes that they'd be wearable when they stopped tumbling.

As she thought through it, Scott continued talking. "I haven't sacrificed anything. It may have seemed like I did, but I actually gained a great life. And the reason this all came together is because I followed the four stages to prosperity."

"Four stages? What are those?" asked Alex.

"I shared with you the idea of prosperity through simplicity at our last meeting, and when you follow the right steps, it really is simple. Stage one is to lay the foundation—to come up with a plan. This is where most people fail. Most people never take the time to build the foundation at all. Instead, they just let life happen and pursue the world's plan for them by default. Most people don't have a vision, and according to the Bible, without a vision, the people perish."

Alex interrupted. "But we had a plan, and it involved building my business, which we've done."

"Exactly—you had a business plan. Most people simply focus on their career or business, though, and never take the time to come up with a *life* plan. I have a Lifeonaire vision for my life. I actually went to a three-day workshop where they helped me develop a vision for my life. It wasn't something that I could just wake up one day and do. Basically, you design your life first and then you build a business or career to fit into your life. Prior to this, I built a business and tried to live life in the time that was left, if any. Life was forced and strained."

"No kidding," said Kerry. "It makes me tired just thinking of how much we have to force the important things in life. I would sure love for it to be more natural."

"It can be when you have a clear life vision. Most people will spend more time planning a weekend getaway or a party than they will their life. That's why the three-day event was so important to me. It forced me to get out of my day-to-day routine and focus on my life, something I had never really done before."

"So where do you go for such an event? I'm sure you don't just look it up in the phone book," Alex joked carefully, still feeling a twinge of pressure from the healing rib on his side.

"They have events in various locations a handful of times throughout the year. I'm going back again next month for my annual tune-up. But let me tell you why it's so important. Your vision becomes the new set of rules that you live by. You can plan and take action when you have a life vision in place. Without a plan, you'll wander aimlessly."

"Now that's something I can relate to," Kerry exclaimed. "In many ways I do feel like someone lost, always wandering around, trying to find my way."

"Well, this is so important because it affects how we live in stage two. Stage one is creating your vision; stage two is where we make ends meet. It's the stage that we must be successful in, or we'll get stuck running on the hamster wheel. This is where most Americans find themselves—stuck," Scott explained, adding a little passion to his words. "When we have no life vision, most of us live life like the game LIFE, by default. We strive to be the winner by accumulating the most. This path makes winning in stage two nearly impossible."

"That's where we're at right now," Alex noted.

"Yes," Scott agreed, "but let me explain more. You see, most people skip stage one altogether. And when they do this, they're setting themselves up to lose the game. Not only do they not know what the rules of the game are if they've never taken the time to write them, they also don't know what would have to happen to win the game either. This is why people go out and create bigger and bigger lifestyles for themselves. They don't even know what they *really* want, so they go out and try to get more to fill the void."

"I think I've done this quite a bit," Alex admitted, looking at his wife. "It's where half of my toys came from. Don't get me wrong, I love my four wheelers and all of that fun stuff, but I don't even have time to enjoy those things and yet I'm still always wanting more."

"And there's nothing wrong with having those things, just as long as we haven't traded our life for them," Scott explained. "We must not only learn to put things in the right perspective, they also need to be put in the right order. Just remember, stage two is where we trade our time for money. The more money you need, the more you're trading your life and time to make those ends meet. We create lifestyles that require us to spend our life forced to earn money to sustain them. If we choose to live simply, though, it makes it much easier to win in stage two. You require less in terms of money, so you spend less in terms of your life and time, and you gain more in terms of your freedom. It's a trade-off.

"Kind of like my Mercedes," Kerry added, catching on. "I do love driving it, but it requires me to go to work every month so that we can continue to make the payment. Maybe that's one of the things holding me back from being home to spend more time with Heather rather than sending her off to the babysitter every day."

Scott beamed, excited to see Kerry understanding. "That's right, just keep in mind that this doesn't necessarily mean you have to live like a pauper out in a tent somewhere. But the more simple your stage two needs are, the faster you can get beyond this stage and on your way to experiencing the true prosperity that comes in later stages. The greater your needs are in stage two, the more difficult it is to get beyond this stage to where all the fun happens. True prosperity comes after you've conquered stage two, so I chose to make some decisions that most people would call drastic in an effort to get beyond this stage as quickly as possible."

Alex and Kerry looked at one another in agreement; they could see the rationale in what he'd said and were starting to understand the idea of the trade-off. "There is no reason why we should be struggling with the income that I make. If we still lived the way we did when we were first married, we would be able to do whatever we want to today. I feel like a fool," Alex muttered, understanding dawning.

"You're no fool, Alex," Scott reassured him. "You've done exactly what you were taught to do, and you did it well. I'm simply introducing you to something different, and if you'll set your mind to it, you'll do this well, also. Setting up the game to win in stage two is critical to being able to move on to stage three. Stage three, after all, is where you make excess cash."

"Right now, we make a lot but never seem to have anything extra," said Kerry.

Scott nodded. "Most Americans make more than they need and could have extra, but they've chosen to spend all, if not more, than they make. Most of the time, this excess is spent on interest payments and maintaining a lifestyle. But if we're careful with stages one and two, then the excess cash that we make in stage three can be used for whatever we want. It can be spent on vacations, donations, used to pay down debt, or whatever, but it should always be used as a tool to get you one step closer to your Lifeonaire vision. It doesn't take long to start seeing big life changes when you're consistently taking steps toward your Lifeonaire vision."

"So at stage three, it sounds like you're already experiencing a great life. What's stage four?" asked Alex.

"Stage four is building a pipeline," Scott answered. "I recommend investing the excess cash from stage three into free and clear income-producing assets. Whether you buy free and clear property, lend money, build a business that makes you cash or even buy or invest into an already existing business, the key is to do it free and clear. If you go into debt to build your pipeline, you'll find yourself serving the lender in stage two again when and if things don't go as planned, trying to make ends meet. Over time, your stage four pipeline will substitute for the time you're currently trading for money in stage two. Meaning, your stage four income starts paying for all of your stage two needs!" Scott leaned forward in his chair excitedly. "This is when you have the ultimate freedom! Winning all four stages gives you more time to experience life and opens up options for you to do whatever you choose to do. I still work because I love to work, but I'm doing something I enjoy. I get paid well for it, but what I get paid is a bonus because I really don't need much. Sounds pretty simple, right?"

Yeah, Alex thought, *maybe not easy, but definitely simple.*

"This is also why the whole "good debt, bad debt' theory has flaws," Scott continued. "You mentioned your rental properties the other day, Alex. Most people think rental properties are a stage four investment, and they can be if they are owned free and clear. But most people don't buy rental properties with cash. They are taught to go out and get a loan for the property, assuming that the tenant will pay for the loan over time with their rent payments. We already agreed that it's possible for one of your rentals to go vacant or that sometimes tenants just don't pay on time, and the so-called 'asset' doesn't perform as planned. When the asset doesn't perform and you still have to pay the lender, you just increased your stage two needs for that month. But, when you have that same rental property free and clear, if something happens and the property goes vacant, there's no lender to serve so your stage two needs don't suddenly increase outside of your control." Scott sat back in his chair and spread his hands wide. "So those are the four stages to prosperity. Create a vision, get your needs met, create excess, build a pipeline."

Alex shook his head in amazement. "Like I said earlier, I feel like a fool. You just made it seem so easy." *Why isn't this being taught anywhere else?* he thought with mixed emotions. *Why couldn't I have heard this conversation ten years ago?* "This goes against the grain of what I've learned everywhere else, Scott. Everything I've been taught is being challenged right now, but it makes sense. With a simple plan and a little patience, my life could look much different than it does today."

Scott leaned forward and put a comforting hand on Alex's shoulder. "But the good news is, it's never too late, Alex. You can start doing things right now and realize the fruits of the four stages in a relatively short period of time. But for now, ladies and gentlemen, it's getting late and I need to run. Would you mind meeting at my place next week? I have a deadline coming up, and I'll be working to meet it throughout the week."

I thought he didn't have to work like that, thought Alex. He briefly considered arguing but knew he'd hear it from Kerry later. "Sure. Where exactly do you live?"

"821 Hamilton Avenue. It's at the far end of the street in the cul-de-sac. I've been meaning to invite the two of you over anyway. I've told my wife all about you, so this is a good excuse for me to finally make the introduction." He pulled out a piece of paper and wrote down his address, handing it to Kerry. "Will it be both of you next week? Kerry, it's always nice to see you."

"I'll try—I really will," Kerry answered. "I'm just already over the amount of time I should be taking off."

"Would you rather come after work? I could switch things around it that works better for both of you," Scott offered.

"It would make things easier for me, but are you sure that's not an inconvenience for you?" she asked.

"Not in the least! What time works for you?"

"I finish at four on a Friday, so maybe four thirty?" She turned to Alex. "Does that work for you, too?"

"I think so. I'll make it work," Alex replied.

"Four thirty it is!" Scott smiled as he slid out of the booth. "Looking forward to it."

I think I am, too, Kerry thought. *I think...*

Chapter

7

"Hamilton Avenue, huh?" Kerry asked Alex. "I have no idea where that is." She entered the address into the GPS and watched as a route appeared. They pulled out of the driveway and listened to the voice from the dashboard as it directed them toward downtown.

"Where does this guy live? Is it even safe around here?" Although Kerry had been looking forward to joining Alex, she started having second thoughts about meeting at Scott's house as she watched the row homes and apartment complexes pass by outside her window. This wasn't what she or Alex had expected. This was more like the areas where Alex renovated some of his homes to flip. Eventually, directed by the GPS, they came to an area of modest single-family homes and turned onto a tree-lined street. They followed the street until it ended, pulled in the driveway of Scott's house and looked around.

It wasn't exactly the house they had pictured for a guy who didn't have any debt. In fact, it looked smaller then Alex's workshop, though it wasn't bad. The cape cod-style house had three, maybe four bedrooms, Alex guessed, and it was very well kept up. Neatly groomed flowerbeds framed the porch, which looked freshly painted. Aside from the impeccable maintenance, however, there was nothing special about this home. It certainly didn't seem like the kind of home that a *very successful* person would live in, though Scott came across as one of the most successful people Alex had ever met.

They stepped out of the car and heard music coming from around the back of the house. It seemed vaguely familiar, and Alex was pretty sure he'd heard it at church at some time or another. They were debating whether to knock or head out back when a petite, smiling woman opened the front door and strode across the porch toward them.

She reached out her hand. "Hi! I'm Joy. You must be Alex and Kerry."

"That's us," answered Kerry, shaking Joy's hand and smiling. Alex followed in turn.

"I've heard so much about the two of you. I'm so glad that you could join us. Scott's around back in the shop," Joy explained. "He gets so caught up when he's working with the kids in there—he probably lost track of time again. Come on back."

As they followed Joy down the driveway and around the side of the house, Alex examined it with a real estate eye. It was the kind of house that would sell within days: no chipping paint, hedges trimmed... It was a home that was very well taken care of. Not fancy, but definitely very nice.

Behind the house, the driveway ended in a detached 2-car garage that was obviously set up as a workshop.

Alex and Kerry saw Scott and a pair of teenagers, huddled around a car parked just inside. Scott was leaning into the hood, and though Alex and Kerry couldn't quite hear the conversation, it was obvious that Scott was making the guys laugh.

And they're not even his kids, Alex thought, judging them to both be at least a couple years older than Justin. *I can't remember the last time I made Justin laugh, much less just hung out with him. And I'm not sure he's ever enjoyed spending time with me...those guys seems to be having a blast.*

Scott turned, saw Joy approaching with Alex and Kerry, and gave a sheepish wave. He glanced at his watch and shrugged. "Time flies out here. I'd shake your hands, but..." He extended his hands, palms-up, to reveal a map of grease smudges, and then gestured toward the guys next to him, similarly spotted with grease. "This is Evan and Josh. They've been teaching me a few new tricks." The two teens seemed to stand a little taller with this introduction.

"Nice to meet you," Evan offered.

The four exchanged greetings, and Scott tossed a pair of rags toward his amateur mechanics. "Nice work, guys—looks like we're done with the hard part. Now, make it shine!" The guys smiled and whipped each other with the rags a few times before turning their attention back toward the car.

After washing up in the slop sink just inside the workshop, Scott and Joy escorted Alex and Kerry across the backyard into the house. As he stepped in, Alex saw that the inside was as welcoming as the outside. "Make yourselves at home," Scott instructed, nodding toward the living room. "Can I get you something to drink? Water? Soda? Iced tea?"

"I'll just have some water, please," Kerry replied.

"Iced tea please," answered Alex. They settled into the couch by the window and took in their surroundings. The room managed to be both simple yet inviting at the same time. In fact, Alex decided, the house felt like a home. Framed snapshots sat on the mantle and a candle burned on the end table. The furniture was basic but well-made and very comfortable, and Alex and Kerry found themselves sinking into not only the cozy couch but also the atmosphere of the house itself. Alex pondered the effortlessly homely feel. *If I didn't know better, I'd think this place was staged to sell.*

As they were talking, a young couple came down the stairs and waved to Scott and Joy. "See you later!" the young man called.

Scott's voice came from the kitchen. "See you tonight!"

The couple, whom Alex guessed were in their early twenties, saw the unfamiliar pair in the living room and offered a quick "hi" before heading out the front door.

Kerry turned to Alex and whispered, "I thought you said that their kids were about the same ages as our kids!"

"I did," Alex answered. "I don't know who they were."

After a few minutes, Scott and Joy returned with the drinks. They handed the glasses to Alex and Kerry and sat next to one another in the loveseat.

"So who was that?" Alex asked Scott.

"Oh, that was Kevin and Shannon," Scott explained. "They got married not too long ago and we're letting them stay here for a while so they can focus on their marriage rather than getting all wrapped up in the rat race. We met them a while back at church when they were just starting college. When they decided to stay in the area after graduating, we felt God nudge us to offer them a room. We were a little doubtful they'd say yes— they are newlyweds after all! But they accepted and so far it's worked out really well. Joy and I have been trying to teach them what we've learned about building a strong relationship, as well as about living abundant lives. We didn't get off to the best start as a couple, and we wanted to do what we could to help another couple do it right from the beginning." Scott smiled at Joy and reached for her hand.

"Wow—I had no idea that you were running a mini Dr. Phil house!" Alex joked, this time realizing he barely even noticed the right side of his ribcage which would have knocked him to his knees just a week earlier. "Seriously, though, that's really cool of you."

Scott smiled. "Well, it does remind me how old I am, that's for sure!"

They all laughed, and Alex took a sip of his drink. "Great iced tea!"

"It's Joy's," Scott said, giving her hand a squeeze. "She makes it better than anyone." Joy smiled and turned an ever-so-slight shade of red.

"Well, my compliments," said Alex, taking another swig. Still, as good as the tea was, he couldn't get one question out of his mind: "So, sorry to sound nosy, but you really don't have a mortgage on this place?"

"Nope," Scott answered. "It's 100 percent ours."

Alex raised his eyebrows and shook his head. "Good for you, man. It's a nice place. Most people don't take care of their houses like this until they're trying to sell them."

"I have Joy to thank for that. I can fix things, but my idea of decorating is to throw a bandana on a random piece of furniture and call it a day."

Joy laughed. "It's true. When I first saw his apartment when we were dating, the only decorations he and his roommate had bothered with was this ratty old bandana on the coffee table."

Kerry smirked and the two women shared look of understanding with each other.

"Seriously, though, we want to know how this whole debt-free thing works," said Kerry once the giggles had died down. "We understand how owing money controls your life, but practically, how can you avoid it? I mean, you obviously have that with your house…"

"But we're not in the position to just buy a house outright," Alex completed her thought.

"How much of your own money is invested in your house?" asked Scott.

"I scraped together about $50,000 when we bought the lot, the rest was a construction loan," said Alex.

"That would have been enough to buy this home. We've done a good bit to it over the last few years, so we have a little more than that into it at this time. But who says you're supposed to own a home?" challenged Scott.

"A lot of people," answered Alex. "Practically every financial expert we've ever heard has said that home ownership is the best investment you can have."

"Well, if investing were the goal of life, then that might make sense. But let's just assume for now that you want to buy a house. How long would it take you to save for it so that you wouldn't have to borrow any money?"

Alex furrowed his brow. "I'd be retired by the time I could save up that much."

"For the house you live in now or one like mine?" Scott prodded.

Alex thought. "I was thinking about mine, but if I were to focus on something smaller in a different part of town, I could do it much sooner."

"Exactly. But do you consider this a bad area of town?"

"Well, uh, not bad, I mean your place is really nice," Alex flushed. "Admittedly, we were a little surprised that you lived here, though. It's not exactly what we were expecting," he tried to explain.

"But this part of town is great. Seriously, the people might not make as much as the people on the other side of town, but they're great people. We love our neighbors, and we don't feel like we have to 'keep up with the Joneses' all the time. Just think of what this part of town would look like if everyone took their $50,000 down payments and bought homes free and clear here." Scott looked at Alex a moment then added, "I'll bet you didn't know that John Robertson lives around the corner." Alex felt his jaw drop open, and Scott nodded and continued.

"He has a real passion for kids. He's been paying for kids' college expenses for many years, but he always just wrote checks from afar. As he's learned how to pursue the Lifeonaire philosophy, he's gotten more excited about investing his money in the lives of youth and investing his time as well. He moved here to get to know the kids he was giving scholarships to, and now he's able to give more with all the money he saves."

"So how long did it take you to save up to buy this home?" asked Kerry, changing the subject slightly. She didn't want Alex to get on the subject of John Robertson; it always derailed him into thoughts of doing business.

That wasn't what they were here for.

"Depends how you look at it," Scott answered. "We said we were saving for quite a while before we really took steps so that we could put more than just a few dollars away at a time. Once we really committed to it—which meant radical changes in our lives, including moving into an apartment, getting rid of cable, buying older vehicles for cash, and selling everything we had with a payment on it—we were able to buy this place in about three years. But when we bought it, it certainly didn't look like it does now. We've put a lot of time and sweat into it over the years."

Alex couldn't hide the fact that he was impressed. "Wow. I've never heard of anyone doing that..." He eyed the room as he had before and tried to picture what the rest of the debt-free house looked like.

"Would you like a look around?" asked Scott, seeming to read Alex's mind.

"We'd love it!" chimed in Kerry. Alex nodded in agreement.

They rose and followed Scott and Joy into the kitchen. It was much smaller than the one in their home but was still more than suited for whipping up anything from a quick snack to Thanksgiving dinner. Alex and Kerry would normally have felt a sense of pride over how nice their home was compared to this, but this time, something was different. What Scott and Joy had was certainly adequate—more than adequate—and it just felt right. Instead of pride, Alex and Kerry felt a conviction, one that spoke to them: *We have so much. Perhaps too much.*

"When we moved in, there was a wall here," Scott explained, motioning to the space between the kitchen and dining room.

"Not to mention that the kitchen was really dated, but it was functional. We saved up and redid this all after about a year of living here—I wanted to be able to talk to my guests when I had them over. This new layout really opened things up," Joy continued.

How long has it been since I had friends or family over? Kerry wondered, looking around her. She couldn't remember the last time they'd had anyone over to enjoy their house. They were always too busy to plan or execute something like that. *Just imagine having a small, intimate setting, where friends and family could hang out,* she thought, *and the time to do it.* Another piece of the puzzle clicked into place for her.

"Of course, it also opens things up if I can keep the counters clear—I have a weakness for kitchen gadgets, but the only ones I really use regularly are the coffeepot and the toaster. I've found that if it's not out, I rarely need it. My mixer fits in a drawer, so it's not hard to get to, but keeping things simpler has really made things easier. It's definitely easier to keep clean," Joy continued with a laugh.

"Easy to clean is always good in my book!" Kerry thought of her own counters, which were cluttered with everything from an espresso machine to a panini press. They definitely weren't easy to clean. Her kitchen didn't look nearly this open. "I love the big windows in here, too," she added.

"That was one of the only features we liked when we first looked at this house," Joy agreed. "It's nice to have lots of light in here in the morning—it helps the coffee work better."

How long has it been since I drank coffee at home with my wife? Alex wondered. He couldn't even remember what the morning light looked like in his own kitchen.

They continued to follow Scott and Joy through the house, past a computer alcove off the living room, and then heading upstairs to see each of the four bedrooms. Joy cringed as she opened the door to Chris's room. "He calls it 'creative,' but it just looks messy to us," she said sheepishly. "He has to clean it once a week, but it seems to revert back to whirlwind state at superhuman speed."

"I guess Justin is 'creative,' too," Kerry laughed, looking at Alex. These bedrooms weren't nearly as big as the bedrooms their own children had, but Alex and Kerry had a feeling that the kids didn't mind one bit.

They headed back downstairs onto the deck and into the yard then. Scott and Alex seemed gravitationally pulled to the shop, while Joy and Kerry wandered over by the gardens.

"I had a feeling they'd end up back there before too long," Joy said, motioning toward the shop.

"It doesn't surprise me one bit," responded Kerry, looking over at the men. "We have a shop in our garage at home, but Alex never gets to actually use it. He's always too busy. I know he'd love to putter around in there, though."

"Scott was always busy, too, for the longest time," Joy replied, nodding. "The funny thing is that when we lived in a bigger house that had a bigger shop, he never used it. We bought that place with a lot of things in mind that we'd do, but in reality, all it turned out to be was a place to sleep when we weren't working."

"That sounds familiar. We chose a house with a huge deck and an outdoor kitchen, thinking it would be nice to cook outside and entertain there, but most nights, we don't even eat together. I try to sit down with the kids, but Alex is only home for dinner once in a while."

"Was it always that way?" asked Joy.

"No, not always, but it's been this way for a while, since before the kids were born," Kerry said, sighing.

• • •

Meanwhile, in the shop, the teens were gone, and Alex and Scott were having a similar conversation.

"I've got a shop like this at home—actually it's a little bigger—but I never use it. I just don't have the time," Alex admitted wistfully, looking around him. "You actually use yours."

"I didn't always," Scott clarified. "Our old place had an even bigger shop, but I never had time to use it. Then we decided to start saving and get a place we could afford. Made that life change. We sold the big place, moved into a small apartment, saved like crazy, and got this place. Now I have a smaller shop, but I actually get to use it, and that makes it all worthwhile."

"You're a rare breed, Scott—most of the guys I know who claim they like to work on cars or build things haven't done it since college."

"Well, how many people do you know that are living an abundant life—the kind of life we've been talking about?" asked Scott.

Alex thought…and thought, finally saying, "The only one I can think of is you…and Joy, of course."

"And how much do you really know about how we live? We've known each other for years, but you don't really know me and understand how I live, do you?"

"True…I guess I just assumed that you were going for the same thing I was," said Alex sheepishly.

"Considering that the vast majority of people are working toward the same goals, that's not surprising. From most people's perspectives, you followed the rules to a T. You've played the game, Alex, and you've played it well. The only problem is that you were playing the wrong game—the one where you get on the hamster wheel and never really get anywhere. The hamster wheel might get nicer and bigger, but it's still a hamster wheel, keeping you running but never taking you forward." Scott took a deep breath and continued. "It was that way for me."

"You're really lucky, though," Alex said. "You have a good life and you made great choices—you don't have to deal will all the bad ones you already made like I do."

"That's not completely true," admitted Scott, shaking his head. "I've made some pretty bad choices, and my life wasn't always like it is now—far from it. Sure, I was successful—quite successful in most people's eyes. But I didn't feel that way at all. I was playing the game by the world's rules, just like you have been. I didn't have a good foundation—not like we're trying to give Kevin and Shannon. I just jumped in and starting doing all I could to get the cash rolling in. It seemed like the right thing to do at the time. I had no idea that my plan was so out of order. I was trying to get rich without a plan for what I wanted to do with my wealth or my life.

"My business was thriving, but I worked all the time—I had no time for life, and I had no idea what I even wanted my life to look like. Everyone said I was a success, but when I stared at the ceiling each night, trying to fall asleep, I didn't feel successful," Scott told Alex solemnly. "Something was missing, but I didn't know what it was. I thought I was doing something wrong and felt like I needed to work harder or do more. I figured if I got to a certain point, then maybe I'd feel successful. My focus was on my work and like I've been telling you, this made me a slave to money. Pursuing it was my only purpose in life."

Scott sat on a stool and pulled another one out a few feet away for Alex. Alex sat, intent on Scott's words.

"But it seems like you were able to put all that past you," Alex reasoned. "How do you do it? I mean, you have it all together now. How did you get to be such a great husband and father if you were approaching life the wrong way?"

"I'm humbled that you think that, but I'm really not the great family man you seem to think I am. I'm the way I am today because I was a terrible father." Alex looked at him quizzically as Scott continued. "What you don't know about me is that I have a twenty-one-year-old daughter, Jessica. Do you remember my girl-friend back in high school, Susy?"

Alex searched his brain and finally nodded. He had a vague recollection of the girl, though they hadn't been very close. He hadn't thought of her in years.

"Not long after we graduated, we had a child together. We were just nineteen. But because of my stu-pid decisions back then, I still struggle to have a rela-tionship with my daughter today." His voice caught and Scott was quiet for a few moments before he continued. "When Jessica was born, I ruined my relationship with her before it even started. I never spent time with her, and as a result, I hardly knew her. To this day, she thinks of me as the jerk who knocked up her mother and left her to raise a child on her own." He could no longer hold back the tears. "And she's right—that's who I was, and there's nothing I can do to change how I hurt her."

Wow. I guess he's not quite as perfect as I thought, Alex thought, suddenly feeling sympathy for the man. "I'm sorry, man—I had no idea," he said, still processing this new way of seeing his friend.

Scott continued quietly. "You'd think I would have learned from my mistakes, but I went right down that same path when I married Joy, and when Chris came along. It was obvious to my wife that my priorities were screwed up. My actions said that I loved pursuing money more than I loved her—I put work first every time and fit her in only when it was convenient. Trust me, I can relate to what you're going through." Scott looked Alex in the eyes, and Alex could see the tears he was keeping at bay. "I used to work seventy hours a week. I always said that I was doing it for my kids. If you'd asked me, I would have said that I thought I was doing the right things, but the truth was that I hadn't thought about it at all. I just played the game." The tears were flowing freely now as Scott shared story after story of times he could have been there for his family and wasn't—times he could never reclaim. "The worst thing is that I didn't just keep myself from the life I wanted—I robbed Joy and the kids of the life they wanted."

He could be talking about me. Alex was riveted by that single thought. *I've only ever been to one of Justin's soccer games. He's been playing for three years, and I've been to just one game. How's that for being there for my son? I'm not even sure what Heather is into right now. Dolls? Princesses? I have no idea. I can't remember the last time I sat on the floor next to her and just spent time with my little girl. This is my life, too.* It was like he was seeing snapshots of the past and of what his life would be if he kept going in the same direction. "That's me," he said softly, staring down at the floor. "I can't get the time back either."

Scott looked at Alex knowingly through the tears. "The truth is, I've screwed up as a father and have a second chance. Alex, you don't have to learn those lessons the hard way!" He put one hand on Alex's shoulder and wiped his eyes with the other. "God gave me a second chance. He gave me Chris and then Marie, and through His grace, I was able to learn to love Joy like she deserved to be loved. I didn't deserve it. I was a screwup in all the things that really mattered."

Alex was fighting tears now—a very rare thing for him. The idea of losing the time with his family—and not being able to get it back—was nearly overwhelming. He had to find a way to keep that from happening. No matter what it took.

"Please, man. Don't wait as long as I did to be the husband and father you need to be. It's simply a choice," Scott pleaded.

Alex nodded, and a tear slipped out, but he didn't say anything. It was as if he saw a fork in the road ahead and suddenly understood that he'd have to choose which path to take. "So what did you do? How did you go from where you were to where you are now?" he asked softly, looking up finally.

Scott took a breath as he regained his composure. "Well, I already told you about how a relationship with God made all the difference in how I view my goals in life, and that's what really changed the decisions I made. But practically speaking, I had to step up and make a plan. Remember those four stages to prosperity I mentioned?"

"Of course—I've been paying at least a little attention, you know."

"Well, I had to go all the way back to stage one to make a plan. I went to a Lifeonaire retreat to help me come up with a vision for my life. At the time, I was making more than I ever thought I would, but almost all of it was going right toward our bills. I knew that I wanted to spend more time with my family, but to live my vision, I'd have to have more time. The problem is, there are only 24 hours in a day. So I had a decision to make. I could either start making a whole lot more money in less time than I was currently working, or I could choose to start cutting expenses. While I knew that making more money was possible, I also realized that the only thing I really have control over is how much I'm spending. Constantly trying to make more money at any expense is what led me to the point where I was working so many hours in the first place. Because my vision was more important to me, I wanted to start living it as quickly as humanly possible. So I made the decision to begin to massively cut our expenses. I took a hard look at what we were spending and found ways to spend less. At first, the cuts were all small, fairly painless things, like going out to dinner less often. Then, decided I would stop trading up into a new car every year or two. Joy did, too. Like you, I was hesitant to go too radical at first. But I began to see that to really put an abundant life over accumulating wealth, we needed to get rid of all our debt, not just have less of it. That's when we put our house on the market. It sold after a few months, and we were able to pay off our mortgage. We moved into an apartment, one that cost us less than half of what we'd been paying for our old place, I'm not going to lie." He looked at Alex steadily. "I'm not suggesting what I did was easy. It was one of the hardest decisions I ever had to make. But I finally came to the conclusion that my life-my families lives-and what was in our Lifeonaire visions-were more important to me!"

Alex was silent, but his mind was racing. *This really is me! I never thought I'd make this much, but now that I am it's always a struggle. And I'm dragging my family into it.*

"After living in the apartment for a few years," Scott continued, "we had saved up enough money to buy this place without a mortgage, even with me working fewer hours. It was always temping to spend our money on other things rather than putting it away for a house, but this time, we had a goal and a plan to keep us on track."

I never had a vision. Alex thought. *I had goals, but what good are goals if they're not in line with my vision? That's why it was never enough. Scott changed...could I really change, too?*

Scott went on, "Now, life is pretty easy. I work, but it's not my whole life. I don't have any debt, so all I really need to make is enough to pay for our utilities, food, and to take care of the house and the car. Anything above and beyond that, I can save or give to whomever I choose. And since I don't need to work all the time, I can spend my time on the things that are important to me." He gestured vaguely to the workshop they were in.

"I used to make the game of life so hard to win, but now it's easy to win because I changed the rules. And I've never been happier. How I felt when I was 'successful' doesn't come close to how I feel now. I do make much more then we need, and Joy and I could move into a larger home and pay cash for it, but we really like our simple life now. We're free, and that feeling is incredible."

Alex was finally starting to hear, not just with his ears, but with every part of him. *For the first time, I think I might actually believe that—not just about Scott, but about me, too, if I could change.* "So how do I get back to stage one when I skipped it twenty years ago? I know we need to set other goals or I'm still going to be struggling to make ends meet when Kerry and I are seventy. I'm just not sure how to do that since I skipped it when I should have done it years ago. It would have been so much easier then!" Alex groaned.

"It would have," Scott agreed, nodding his head, "but don't beat yourself up over that. I didn't start off with goals either. And like you, I was stuck at stage two because I allowed the world around me to write the rules for abundant living. You're attempting to build wealth, but you've gone about it backward. You never made ends meet before you added more to your lifestyle. So instead of building wealth, you're building debt. You've been playing the same game as everyone around you, so you and Kerry have set yourselves up to lose."

"We're starting to see that," replied Alex. "It's just not nearly as simple as it could have been for us. But I can see what you mean about starting from the ground and working our way back up. Being more in control of our path this time. Making our lives simpler. I paid more in taxes last year than I made in a year when we were first married. And I've never stopped finding ways to grow my lifestyle with my salary."

"It almost always works that way. It's like putting a fish in a bigger tank—the fish won't get excited that it has more space. It will grow in proportion to the tank," Scott explained.

Alex wrinkled his forehead. "I see what you're getting at, but you can't just put the fish back in the smaller tank once it's grown. How can I make what I used to earn seem like a lot again or at least enough? It's like… it would be like trying to convince yourself that powdered iced tea is wonderful when you're used to drinking Joy's homemade tea. How can you go back?"

"Well, let's imagine that you didn't need to pay taxes this year—that you had $40,000 to spare," Scott suggested. "Would it seem like more then, if it was yours to do with as you chose?"

"Of course. It would be mine to keep," Alex answered.

"Exactly. Having more than you need isn't about how much you make. It's not how much you bring in, but how much you bring in compared to how much you need. I'm rich because I don't need much and I make more than I need. I've set myself up to win."

Kerry's voice interrupted their conversation. "Alex? Did you get lost back here?" She and Joy were standing in the open doorway, smiling at their husbands.

"I'm here," he called.

"I hate to say it, but it's getting late and we're going to have to leave soon," said Kerry.

"Coming," Alex said, glancing down at his watch. The two men joined their wives and they headed back into the house.

"What kind of trouble were the two of you getting into out there?" Joy asked jokingly, looking at Scott with narrowed eyes as they all gathered in the kitchen. She collected their empty glasses and placed them in the sink to be washed later.

"No trouble at all…" replied Scott, innocently. "That you know of!"

"Uh huh. I've heard that one before," said Joy. "I know what happens when boys get together in a garage. What I'd give to be a fly on the wall…"

Alex jumped in, "All kidding aside, Joy, it's actually nice to know that other men sometimes struggle with the same things I do. Thanks Scott, for being so completely open with me."

"Any time, my friend. Any time."

Kerry smiled at Alex but said, "This has been great and I really wish we could stay, but it's almost six thirty. We need to leave to pick up Justin. He had an away game tonight, remember?"

"I remember. We do need to leave." He turned back to Scott, smiling. "Could we continue this next week?"

"Sure. That'd be great."

The four of them walked outside, chatting quietly about their plans for the weekend. "See you at church on Sunday?" Scott asked them, once again.

Kerry answered this time. "We can't this Sunday— Justin has a soccer game in the morning. Maybe next Sunday? Justin has a game that day, too, but it's a little later." She looked at Alex questioningly.

"I think we can try for that," he answered.

"It would be great to see you there," said Joy. "Regardless, it was great to see you here! Thanks for coming!"

"Thanks for having us," answered Kerry, smiling at her new friend.

"And for showing us around," added Alex.

With a wave, they headed toward their car. When they were a block away, Kerry asked, "What were you guys talking about in the shop, really?" She wasn't quite sure what she saw in Alex's face, but it wasn't a look he wore often.

"We, uh…Scott shared about his past." Alex gave Kerry the abbreviated version, unsure of how much he thought Scott would want him to share. Kerry continued to study her husband's face, taking in just how much the conversation had burned into his brain. Perhaps there was something there, she thought; some light bulb had come on. He hadn't really understood before, but now he did, or at least seemed to.

"What did you and Joy talk about?" Alex asked.

Kerry smirked. "Well, for once, we weren't the emotional ones! Actually, we talked about a lot of the same things, except that Joy didn't tell me as much about her past. I think we have more in common with them than we thought. From what Joy said, Scott was a lot like you, and I know I related to her too."

"How so?"

"We just clicked. She seemed to understand when I told her how I felt like we didn't have a choice and that we have to live the way we do because we've already chosen it. But, like Scott, she also told me that I had a choice—that it wasn't too late for us to start changing the rules of the game."

• • •

Kerry felt like they needed to go to church on Sunday, even if they couldn't stay the entire time, and Alex agreed with her. She told Justin to get dressed for his soccer game and got everyone into the car and on their way. Pulling into a spot in the church parking lot and climbing out of the car, they saw Scott and his family doing the same just a few rows over. Alex waved and the two families met in front of the church doors.

"Hey! Nice to see you!" Scott greeted them cheerfully. Alex and Kerry smiled sheepishly, and Justin traced a line in the pavement without answering. After a moment of shaking hands and introducing Justin and Heather to Joy and her children, they all followed Scott inside and found a seat.

As the opening song began and the people around him stood up, Alex's mind fluttered around the idea of being there and the lyrics of the song. Though he'd been to church plenty of times before, he wasn't sure what made him come this time. After all, it wasn't Easter or Christmas! For some reason, church was a lot like going to the gym for Alex. He never really minded it once he was there, but for some reason getting there always seemed like the hard part. Maybe part of it was that by the time Sunday came around, he was so tired from working all week that he just didn't feel like doing much of anything. Like there was no more left in him to even make an effort to get there.

After a few announcements, a video clip began to play on the big screen above the stage, one that showed a single mother in the church who needed a car. The woman in the video, Angela, had three kids and had been taking all of them, including the baby, on the bus. Her husband died in a car accident just before their third child was born, and she was struggling to make ends meet. Her husband had been the breadwinner and when he died, they had just enough money saved up to cover the funeral expenses. When the engine on their car blew up just a few months earlier and she couldn't afford to repair it, Angela was at the lowest point of her life. When the clip ended, the pastor called the woman up to the pulpit. Her face was painted with equal parts anticipation, sadness and confusion.

As she reached the front, the pastor reached under the pulpit and began to speak. "Hi, Angela. I'm guessing that story looked a little familiar?" She nodded, eyes wide. "Well, I have the next chapter right here—and in the parking lot." He raised his hand to reveal a set of keys as a picture of a car appeared on the screen—a car that looked very familiar to Alex- the car that he had seen in Scott's workshop just two days before.

Angela's hands flew over her mouth and tears began to flow. The pastor put his arm around her as he spoke to the congregation. "Those of you who are regulars here know that this isn't the first time that someone in need has received a car. We have a very generous individual in our church—one who prefers to remain anonymous—and we're very grateful for the ability to reach out in this way." He turned back to Angela, who was still trying to catch her breath. "Angela, enjoy your new car!"

The sanctuary burst into applause, and congregants from teens to senior citizens began wiping tears from their eyes as they shared Angela's joy. Alex felt his own eyes grow moist as he clapped, and he saw Kerry grab a tissue from her purse. Even Justin looked moved; though he wasn't crying, his eyes were fixed on the stage, and Alex caught him biting his lip. Heather, of course, was doing little more than squirming on Kerry's hip, though Alex fancied he saw her looking around at the suddenly excited congregation.

And then he looked right and saw Scott. Like the rest of the church, he was applauding vigorously and his face was wet with tears of joy. To anyone else, he would have looked like everyone else there—a jubilant observer rather than the one behind the gift, but Alex knew better. He gave Scott a little punch in the air and a "Way to go, man!" look. Scott grinned at him quickly and fixed his eyes on Angela's radiant face once again.

Kerry nudged Alex and discretely pointed across the aisle at the two young guys they'd seen in the garage working on the car. They gave off a sense of pride as they clapped and cheered but didn't give anything away.

Just as the applause was dying down and Angela took her seat, Alex's phone buzzed in reminder of Justin's soccer game. *Now? Of all times!* He tapped Kerry on the shoulder and she tapped Justin, who looked equally disappointed at the prospect of leaving. "Soccer game," Alex mouthed to his son, and Kerry gave him the "mom" look as she took Heather's hand in hers.

They excused themselves as gracefully as they could and squeezed past Scott and his family.

"See you next week?" Scott whispered as they passed. All three nodded.

• • •

The week seemed to drag. Although Alex was certainly busy enough, his thoughts kept wandering back to Angela's face at church on Sunday...and to Scott's face when he had seen her reaction to his anonymous gift. Had he ever been that happy, Alex wondered? By the time Friday came around, he couldn't wait to talk to Scott about it.

"Man, that was some gift you gave on Sunday!" he exclaimed to Scott as he sat down at the coffee shop, before even trying his coffee. "I can't get her face out of my mind. I wish I could give like that!"

"Who says you can't?" countered Scott, taking a sip of his own drink.

"My bookkeeper, for one. You give a lot because you have a lot. It's not hard for you to give," Alex insisted.

"Alex, you're making an assumption again. I've never told you how much I make," Scott countered.

"Well, no, but—"

"The reason I have money is because I don't have debt and my stage two needs are very simple. When I make it, I get to keep it. And I can emphatically say that I don't give a lot because I have a lot, I have a lot *because* I give a lot," Scott explained. "I'm using my money the way that God wants me to use it, and He trusts me with more. Alex, one of the greatest joys of my life is being able to bless others—it truly is. It gives me this deep satisfaction that I could never buy, no matter how much I made, and because of this I choose to live a lifestyle in which I'm free to give. I'd really appreciate it if you never tell anyone what you saw in my workshop last week. I get the most joy when those I'm able to help simply know that they've received a gift from God."

Alex nodded his understanding. "No problem—my lips are sealed."

"Thanks. I really do appreciate that. I can think back years ago to times when I was able to help people, and it still brings me tears of joy. They still have no idea where it came from, and they'll probably never know. There's just no feeling like it, and I'd never do anything to compromise my ability to give. That's the reason I live without debt." Just thinking back brought a goofy smile to Scott's face.

"I'd like to give, too," Alex declared. "I really hope I have enough money one day that I can."

"But you can now," Scott countered. "You don't have to wait. It's sort of like Justin's camping trip. If it were as much a priority as one of your business meetings, you'd figure out a way to make it happen. Up to this point, it just hasn't been a priority to you." He looked at Alex steadily.

"Man, you make it sound so easy," Alex grumbled. "It just feels like I would have to give up so much right now to be able to give like that. You don't have to give up much of anything to be generous because of where you are now. I'm not there yet."

Scott shook his head. "Have you ever heard the phrase 'He who can be trusted with little can be trusted with much'? You would never give one of your employees more responsibility if they haven't properly managed the responsibilities you had already given them, right? The same principle applies here, my friend. If you won't give when you don't have much to give, you won't give when you have more. The key to giving is to start giving *now*, even when you feel you don't have much to offer. This brings me to our final principle and that principal is to *share life*. When you sow life you will reap life. The rewards of giving so that someone else can experience a great life are incredible." Scott smiled at Alex across the booth. "Giving no longer feels like a sacrifice to me, but it wasn't always that way. Trust me, I know it's hard to start. But you'll always find ways to spend money, no matter how much you make. And you'll always find ways to give when you make that a rule of your game."

Alex stared at the table. He couldn't argue, but he wasn't quite sure how to agree either. "I see what you're saying—I think it's true. But right now, it seems impossible, or like believing in the impossible. I want to be able to give, but I don't know if I can give up anything to do it. Can we get together again—all four of us—to talk about this? I think this is something Kerry and I need to think through together."

"Sure. Actually, how about the two of you come over for dinner next Friday night?" Scott offered. "I'll have to double-check with Joy, but I'm pretty sure we're not doing anything else that night."

"That would be great. I'll double check with Kerry, too—I've learned the hard way not to make plans that involve both of us without talking to her first," Alex chuckled. "That never ends well."

"I hear you! How about we plan on Friday at six thirty pending wife approval?" Scott suggested.

"Sounds like a plan."

• • •

It hadn't been a fancy meal, but it was one of the best Alex and Kerry had eaten in a while. They could smell the grilled chicken as soon as they got out of the car, and it proved to taste as good as it smelled. Joy had served it up with roasted potatoes and a big salad and treated them all to peach cobbler.

Of course they couldn't help but talk about the car giveaway again. Kerry especially raved about their generosity, even though getting credit seemed to make Scott and Joy a little uneasy. They were still on the topic of giving when the group moved into the living room after dinner.

"All week, we've been talking about different ways we'd like to give once we have enough money," bubbled Kerry to Joy. "We want to buy computers for the community center, give to cancer research, and maybe even help to pay for a disadvantaged college student's tuition. Seeing the joy that giving has brought you and Scott has made us excited to plan to do the same thing someday."

"Even seeing it as just observers brought us joy," added Alex. "Imagine if we were the ones doing the giving!"

"Yeah, we can't wait to be able to experience that for ourselves." Kerry agreed.

"Have you ever done anything that's brought you that kind of joy?" asked Joy.

"Well..." Alex wasn't sure. With just a glance at Kerry, he knew that she wasn't sure, either.

After an awkward silence and a few sips of their iced tea, Kerry spoke up. "There was this time we paid for a kid from a less affluent family to go to the summer camp that Justin goes to each summer."

Alex lit up. "That's right! I forgot about that! Seeing that boy's face was the highlight of our summer."

Kerry grinned at him, remembering. "It was! He was so surprised! He'd never ridden a horse or cooked over a fire and knowing that because of us he had a whole week of those experiences was one of the best feelings." Both she and Alex were beaming. "I'm getting goose bumps just thinking about it!"

"I am, too!" exclaimed Alex, starting to laugh. "Look at us—we're both talking like my grandmother!" he chuckled, referencing a woman who was animated until the day she died.

"We are!" laughed Kerry. "We haven't used our hands to talk this much since we both had laryngitis! We look alive for once!"

"I can't believe we forgot about that—it felt so good knowing we helped that boy. It still makes us feel good, obviously," said Alex.

"We haven't thought about that in a long time," admitted Kerry, still half smiling, lost in the memory. "We really should do that more often—a lot more often." Alex nodded in agreement, and she continued. "But that's going to have to come later in life. I mean, we can't get out of debt and give at the same time."

Alex grimaced slightly, knowing what was coming from Scott.

"We talked about that a bit last week, didn't we Alex?" Scott probed gently.

"Yeah, that's why we're here. You said that when we make giving a part of the rules, we'll always find a way to do it, but that we would need to give something up," Alex answered.

"Exactly," replied Scott. "Most people don't think like that, though. The vast majority of Americans assume that they'll give 'someday' when they have an abundance of wealth, but not until then. The problem is that 'someday' might never come, and they deny themselves the joy of giving while waiting for it. If 'someday' *does* come, the truth is that they aren't going to give then if they didn't give before. If we don't give when we have a little, we aren't going to give when we have a lot because we haven't made giving a part of the rules we live by. Let me ask, did you make as much as you do now when you sent that kid to camp?"

"No," Alex admitted. "I mean, it certainly wasn't during our $40,000-a-year days, but we did make less than…" The dots were coming together on a more personal level.

"I think I get it!" Kerry exclaimed. "It's like when I kept saying for years that I'd exercise 'when.' When Justin was in preschool I'd always say that I'd start when he went to school because I'd have more time. When he went to kindergarten, I said I'd do it when he was in school all day. They put in a gym at work, and I was still making excuses, even though I could walk on the track during my lunch break or take a class right after work without having to drive anywhere. I didn't make working out a priority when I had a little time, so it really wasn't surprising that I didn't do it when I had more time either. It didn't change until I changed the way I looked at it."

"What changed the way you looked at it?" asked Joy.

"Well, wanting to look good for a class reunion had something to do with it," laughed Kerry. "But even more than that, I realized that I was going to be middle aged soon and that I didn't want to wait to get in shape. After all, it was going to get harder the older I got. I knew I wanted to be healthy for my family, but I saw that I'd always find excuses if I kept going the way I was going."

"Well said, Kerry," Scott replied. "Unless we change our plan, we'll just keep going the way we're going, and usually that means that we just keep following the world's plan." He looked at Alex as if to say, "Do you agree?"

Alex was still processing, torn between the ideas he could see forming and the ones he'd lived with for his entire life. "It makes sense. I guess it just doesn't seem practical right now."

"Will it ever seem practical?" asked Scott gently. "Remember how joyful you felt just a few minutes ago? Why deny yourself that? You were able to give when you had less. Why not just do it now?"

"You sound like a Nike commercial," said Alex dryly, not really sure how else to reply—it was a big question.

Scott laughed. "I hadn't thought about it before, but it's not a bad motto for giving, actually."

Kerry spoke up now. "I guess what we're really struggling with isn't whether we *can* give, but that we'd have to deny ourselves things we've worked for to do it. I understand that it's what we need to do to experience life, but…"

Alex jumped in. "We've worked hard for the way we live. It's not like it was handed to us."

"And denying ourselves of what we've worked for just seems wrong," said Kerry, completing his thought.

"I know that feeling, I really do," Joy confessed. "Trust me, I wasn't big on the idea of scaling back. It wasn't like returning a gift—we'd earned our life! I felt like I was robbing myself at first…but then I started to experience the joy that came with giving. Tell me: have the two of you ever experienced the same joy that you felt when you sent that boy to camp?"

Will Kerry strangle me if I don't put our wedding day in that category? Alex wondered. He was let off the hook when she answered first.

"You mean aside from the birth of our children?" Kerry asked jokingly. "No, in all seriousness, yes, but not like that. Not really. Can you think of anything?" she asked, turning the Alex.

He shook his head. "No, I really can't…I mean, don't get me wrong, I can think of a bunch of things I've been excited about in the past. I remember when I did my very first real estate deal. That was an awesome feeling, but it was because I overcame this huge obstacle in front of me and I was excited that I actually pulled it off. I think that's a different kind of joy though, because when I think back to that moment, sure I'm proud of pulling it off but it doesn't bring tears to my eyes. Seeing that kid experience something he never would have without us though, that's a whole different story. When I think about that, I still get shaken up even to this day. I can't think of anything that we're working towards in our lives right now that might bring that kind of joy again."

Scott leaned forward and looked both Alex and Kerry in the eyes. "It's not likely that you'll find anything else that does, when your goal is to make money. By choosing the lifestyle you live, you're actually denying yourselves of this joy—the thing that you really want. I know that giving up things you've worked for seems like denial, but this—missing out on the joy of life—is the real denial. You're depriving yourselves of the ability to experience true joy, and your complicated lifestyle—the very thing you're afraid to give up—is what stands in the way."

Scott reached for his Bible, which was sitting next to him on the end table. "Do you know the story of the rich young ruler?" he asked them.

"It's been a while," Alex admitted. "Uh, not really."

"Let me give you a quick refresher then. I won't make you read the passage for yourself!" Scott laughed before continuing with his story. "Jesus was approached by a rich young ruler, and the ruler asked him what he had to do to inherit eternal life. Simple, right? 'What rules do I have to follow to get there?' Jesus told the ruler that he already knew the commandments—don't commit adultery, don't kill anyone, don't steal, don't give false testimony, and honor your parents. The ruler said he'd followed those commandments since he was a boy. But Jesus could see the young rulers heart and told him that there was one thing that he lacked. Jesus told the young man to sell everything that he had, give it to the poor and then he would have treasure in heaven. Finally Jesus said 'and come follow me."

"I think I remember that story," Alex said slowly, trying to recall. "The ruler didn't like that suggestion much."

Scott shook his head. "You're right, he didn't. He got upset because he was very wealthy, and he didn't want to sell all his things. Most people shutter at this passage and many believe that Jesus would never ask someone to sell everything that they have and to give it away. I don't think Jesus could have been anymore clear. But it is important to know that Jesus was not asking the rich young ruler to deny himself of nice things, Jesus knew that all of his riches were getting in the way of his experiencing life. Jesus wanted to remove the obstacle so that the young ruler could experience real abundance. There is nothing wrong with having nice things, but there is something wrong when nice things have you."

Alex nodded, trying to put the pieces together. "I guess that does sound a little familiar. I feel like I've done all the right things...all the things I've been taught...but in the end, it's not enough. It's not going to give me a good life."

"Alex, you have a lot in common with this ruler. He'd followed the Jewish law all his life, just like you've followed the rules of the game. What he didn't realize was that the law wasn't the point—instead, it was the abundant life Jesus was offering, the same life that both of you have been offered." He paused for a few moments to let them digest and then continued. "This ruler came to Jesus looking for life, but he didn't like Jesus's answer; he misunderstood it. He felt like he was being asked to deny himself of things, but what he was really being asked was to *not* deny himself of life. Jesus asked him to embrace life and to remove the obstacles that were in his way. He asked him to get rid of the things that were weighing him down and move into an abundant life."

Alex didn't say anything, but his mind was racing. *I've been missing the point...I'm just like this guy...I see an opportunity to have what I really want—what I didn't even know I wanted until now—and I'm turning it down because I don't want to give up all I've worked for. I'm choosing to turn down life. I have a choice.*

Scott continued. "Jesus says in John 10:10 that He came so that we could have life and have it abundantly. Jesus wasn't asking the rich young ruler to deny himself but to embrace true life and true abundance. This isn't about deprivation! The young man thought that he could find life and joy in his possessions, and he was upset at the proposition of giving them away. He didn't understand that truth, and he went away sad because of it. And he wasn't the only one who was upset—Jesus was sad, too. He was offering life and He knew that it was possible for the rich young ruler to embrace it. Jesus knew that the rewards of embracing life far outweighed the cost, but that young man couldn't change his thought process to understand that."

Kerry's mind was racing, too. *I know all this...I've known it all for a while. I could never put it into words before. But I'm turning it down. I understand it all—I think Alex does, too—but we still turn it down.*

Alex spoke up. "You're right, man. I am a lot like this guy. I'm turning down life because I think the cost is too great. I've spent so long playing by the same rules as the ruler, and just like him, I don't want to let go of what I've earned because I still think that somehow I can earn joy. It always seemed like the way to go."

"It has to a lot of people for a long time. People have been trying to find life and joy in possessions for thousands of years, and we Americans have honed this pursuit into an art form. We've perfected it, even though it robs us of abundant life."

"So what do we do now?" asked Kerry, looking from Scott to Joy.

"Well, that's up to the two of you," answered Scott, "but I can offer a few suggestions if you're willing to take them." Both Alex and Kerry nodded, and Scott continued, "Let's take a look at your schedule. You're pretty busy, right?"

"That's an understatement," smirked Kerry.

"Well, a lot of that is because your money has mastered you. What do you spend the most time doing?"

"Work," answered Alex. "I'm sure that doesn't surprise you."

"And it's because we have to pay off our debt. Our debt masters us," Kerry added.

Scott smiled. "You *have* been listening. So you can see that your schedule is determined by what you owe, not by what would bring you joy?"

"Yes," sighed Alex. "It's not like I'd work this many hours if I didn't need to. It's not like I want Kerry to have to work. I'd much rather that both of us work less, spend time with each other, and be able to help others, but we can't because of our debt."

"What else does your debt determine?" asked Scott.

Kerry spoke up. "Well, since we're working so much, we can't do other things we'd like to do. I don't spend nearly as much time with the kids as I'd like to. I certainly wouldn't put Heather in daycare if I didn't have to work."

"It definitely affects how we parent. It really affects our marriage too. We don't do much as a couple," added Alex. "Honestly, it's almost surprising we're still married. It's not like divorce has never come up—it's definitely crossed our minds. Weeks can go by where we barely see each other, and when we do, we often fight about it. We fight about money, too. It seems like the more we have of it, the more we argue about it."

"That's really common," said Joy. "Fighting and even splitting up over finances is almost inevitable when your focus is money. We've seen that a lot."

Kerry turned to Alex, nodding. "Just think of all the couples we know who've called it quits because of finances. Zack and Jenny split up last year, Ben and Tamara got divorced right after their son was born…I always thought they were perfect for each other."

"And then there's Martin and Amy," Alex mused. "They'd been married over twenty-five years when we heard that they were getting divorced. They have more money than us, but they were always fighting about it."

Scott jumped back in. "So what's going to stop you from becoming like them?"

"I know the right answer—it's time to make a change," answered Alex. "If we don't change, we *will* end up like them. We have to make time for each other and make living a priority in our life, instead of money.

But life is so busy. There are a lot of things we'd like to do, but we just can't fit them in. I'd love to get more involved in church, and get the kids more involved too-but I can only be in one place at a time."

Scott could sense Alex's growing frustration and decided it was time for a little break. "Since we can only be in one place in one time, do you want to go sit out on the porch? It's a nice night."

"That would be nice," answered Kerry.

"Would you like a refill on your tea on your way out?" asked Joy.

"I'm not going to turn that down," said Alex, handing her his glass. Kerry handed hers over as well, and then they followed Scott outside and settled into a pair of gliders. Joy quickly returned with their drinks and joined Scott on the porch swing.

"So where were we?" he asked.

"Talking about time—or lack of it," Alex said.

"Right. A lot of this comes down to discipline," Scott explained. He turned to Kerry. "When you first decided to make exercising a priority and started working out, was it easy?"

Kerry made a face. "Easy? Are you kidding? I was panting so hard I could have been mistaken for a golden retriever!"

Scott laughed. "It took discipline, didn't it?"

"It sure did! I had to keep at it, even when it was the last thing I wanted to do. It got better eventually, but those first few weeks were hard," she admitted, shaking her head.

"Discipline is really nothing more than a strong belief that what you're doing is actually worth doing. It's a whole lot easier to follow through when your beliefs change. I'm assuming you'd say the workouts are worth it, right?" asked Scott.

"Definitely. I feel better. It's what keeps me motivated. That, and I don't want to have to get back in shape all over again."

"I think I see what you're getting at," Alex interjected. "If we want life, it's going to take discipline. We have to bite the bullet and do it, even though it's going to be hard at first, so we can reap the rewards at the end. And that starts with a belief that it really is worth it."

"I couldn't have said it better," said Scott. "Living abundantly involves doing things you may not initially want to do. It won't be easy at first, but as Kerry illustrated, it's worth it. And much like working out our muscles, this abundance grows over time and gets easier and easier. As difficult as it seems at first, when you stick with it and start seeing the benefits of your new life, you begin to love it so much that it no longer takes the discipline it once did. It's almost as if it becomes engrained in you."

Alex sat back and exhaled. There was no way around it: if they were going to do this, it was going to take some serious work. "I know it's worth it. I'm just not sure how to do it. And if I do know how to do it, I'm really not looking forward to it."

"I'd be a little worried if you did!" said Scott. "A lot of discipline involves setting boundaries, and when we set boundaries, it means that the things outside of those boundaries have to go. If you set a boundary for the number of hours you'll work per week or how late you'll work, then you'll have to say no to certain projects. Or if you set a boundary that dictates how much money you'll spend, you have to forgo the things that are over and above that amount. I'll admit, boundaries aren't the most enjoyable things in and of themselves, but they help us work toward our goals—they help us keep our focus on abundant life, and our vision, rather than on following the rules we've been following all our lives."

Joy jumped in. "I appreciate boundaries most as a mom. I set limits for the kids on how much TV they can watch or how much candy they can have because I know that staying within those limits will be good for them. Seeing it from this perspective helps me remember that God also gives us boundaries for our own good—because He wants us to live life to the fullest."

"I can relate to that," said Kerry. "I know that if I didn't give the kids boundaries for how late they could stay up on a school night, they'd be bouncing off the walls at 2:00 AM! But I also know how miserable they'd be the next day. They think that by going to bed, they're being deprived of the joys of staying up late, but in reality, I'm looking out for them."

"You know," said Alex, "I don't want this to come across wrong, but all that you've taught us is so simple that it kind of irritates me that we aren't already doing it. I think a lot of other people instinctively know this stuff too, but so few act on it. Why don't we choose to live a lifestyle that's centered around abundance? It just doesn't make sense. It seems like it would be so much easier if people learned this earlier, so they didn't have to reset halfway through life."

"You're right—our entire lives we've been conditioned to live like the rest of the world," explained Scott. "We have been taught to pursue money so that we can one day have life. Lifeonaires pursue life every day. As I share what I've learned with others, so many of them still think that they can find joy through things and earn their way to an abundant life. They agree with what I say, but ultimately, they choose a path that doesn't actually lead to life. Very few people choose life."

Scott paused and studied Alex and Kerry's faces. They were painted with a full range of emotions, and the tension couldn't be hidden. He looked at them both and asked, "So, what will it be? Do you have the guts to go against the flow of what everyone else has been telling you? Will you make the hard choices now so you can begin living as a Lifeonaire today? To tell you the truth, when you really know what you want out of life, the choices aren't so hard. The question is-do you have the guts? Will you choose an abundant life?"

Alex and Kerry were reeling, both from the prospect of changing their entire approach to life and about the possibility that they would experience joy as they had in the past. What would it mean to really embrace life rather than playing the game they'd always played? To actually pursue a goal they set rather than going after the goals others had set for them?

"Talk about it," said Scott. "I'm not going to ask for an answer now, but I'll ask again."

"I know you will," said Alex, "and trust me, I don't think we could get through this week without thinking about it. It's probably *all* we'll think about."

Kerry nodded in agreement then peered at her watch. *Ten fifteen!* They had to get back home to the sitter! She nudged Alex. "We've got to go! We told the sitter we'd be back by ten!"

As they stood to go, Scott offered one last invitation. "Hey, Alex, I get together with a group of guys each week who are committed to living as Lifeonaires. It's just a small group of guys who are committed to each other and to sharing the way of life we've found with others. I think you might be ready for something like this if you're interested in joining us. It would be great if you could be a part of it. What do you think?"

If I do this, I'm in all the way, thought Alex. "When do you meet?" he asked.

"Tuesday nights at eight over at the church. It's not technically a church group, but they let us use a room. Think you can make it?"

"I'll try," answered Alex. "I don't think I can this coming up week because I have an appointment already scheduled on Tuesday night, but maybe I can try to shoot for the following week. You still up for meeting again at our usual spot next Friday?"

"I wouldn't miss it. See you Sunday?"

"I think I need these boundaries in place more than you know. I already committed to something on Sunday that I probably wouldn't have if you and I had this conversation a week ago," replied Alex.

"Don't worry, you'll get there... if you've got the guts."

Chapter

8

Alex, now healing up nicely and able to drive again on his own, pulled into Cup of Hope with just one minute to spare, eager to discuss what he and Kerry had talked about over and over that week. He barely got past "hello" before jumping into the topic with Scott.

"Man, you really got us talking this week—especially about boundaries! We even made up a list of limits we want to set to help us pursue an abundant life. Kerry wanted to be here to talk about this, too, but she had to take Justin to a dentist appointment. She'll stop by afterward if it doesn't take too long."

"It would be nice to see her again. So what's on your list?"

"A lot," answered Alex. "No working on Sundays, limiting the work I bring home, boundaries for how much we spend for gifts for the kids...actually, we talked a lot about setting boundaries that will help the kids. I don't want Justin to make the mistakes I've made. I want him to have a good life from the start." Alex realized he was beginning to speak with the same passion he heard in Scott every time he talked about abundant life.

"Alex, what do you really want for Justin?" prodded Scott.

"I want him to be free, to live his life without making the mistakes I've made…" Alex's voice drifted off.

"Well I'm sure he'll make a whole lot of different mistakes as he grows up then, but thank God he won't make yours!" Scott said jokingly. "I don't think it's possible for Justin to grow up without making any mistakes, but I get what you mean. That's a lot different than what you said a couple months ago," Scott observed. "The last time I asked you about this you talked about him being successful—about getting a good job and playing the game just like you did. Your vision for him has changed—but that's not surprising, since your vision for your own life has changed."

"I guess you're right. I still want him to follow in my footsteps in some ways, but my ideas about the steps I should take are changing. I don't want him to go through life without a life vision like I've been doing— I want him to experience life; to live the way I should have been living this whole time." Alex said with a rueful smile. "He has a chance to come up with his own life vision before he makes mistakes and follows in the footsteps of others. I never really sat down to think about planning my life—I certainly never wrote it down. I hope he learns how to do that before it's too late."

"Well, what about writing it down now?" suggested Scott. "When you put your vision for your life into writing, it helps to solidify it. Otherwise, your vision will always be changing, and it'll be next to impossible to have an abundant life. When we take time to clarify our vision, we can come to grips with what it is that we really want. Then we can really go after it in everything we do."

"That makes sense...but I thought we were talking about Justin."

"We are! If you want Justin to know how to have freedom, you have to provide him with a good example. Alex, it's your responsibility to model the life that you want for Justin," Scott reminded him. "Remember when we talked about how he's watching you?"

Alex nodded.

"This is why that's such a big deal! You can help him get on the right track, but only if you're on the right path, too — the path to an abundant life. Until now, you've been following a lot of other paths, and Justin is likely to follow them, too, unless you make a plan for what you want your life—and eventually his life—to look like."

"What about Heather? What do you want for her?" asked Scott.

"I want Heather to know that she doesn't have to settle. She deserves a man that makes her a priority. Up until now, I haven't been a role model for what it means to be that man in her life. I want her to feel unconditional love from her family. I want her to know that she can become anything she chooses to become, and that she doesn't have to settle for anything less than God created her for. She doesn't have to follow the same path her mother and I have. I want her to have the freedom to just be a kid, and grow up with a father who knows her and loves her and spends time with her, all the while showing her that providing means a whole lot more than just finances. It means I need to provide a whole lot more for her than just finances. She needs me emotionally, spiritually, financially, and with my time." Alex spouted off as though reading a well rehearsed speech, though it was pure and genuine, it was as if Alex was finally allowing himself to speak from the heart rather than from his head.

Scott beamed, "Good. Very good. Now you're talking."

"So what do you want your life to look like?" asked Alex, eager to turn the focus of the conversation away from himself for a few minutes. He wasn't quite used to speaking so openly from his heart, and while it felt good to be so open, it was a muscle that hadn't been used regularly and already atrophied.

Scott leaned back and smiled. "I want to be free—I want my whole family to be free. I want to show my children that they can write their own rules for their lives, and that it's okay to go against what society says. I want to be the example for them. I want to be full of life." It was obvious that Scott had given this a lot of thought. His words weren't just off the cuff, but they weren't rehearsed either—they seemed to flow from deep inside of him. "Now, my goal is to live a life that's pleasing to God." Scott was truly beaming now. "It's such a blessing to live this way. I get to build into the lives of so many people! We're helping Kevin and Shannon get a good head start on life together by keeping them from going into debt following the world's plan. So many couples split because of money, and by helping Kevin and Shannon begin to build their lives without debt, we can help them stick together for life. I get to walk with John Robertson and help him keep his focus on his family—to encourage him to honor the commitment he's made and put what he claims is most important to him before everything else. God blesses him with the ability to make money, and he's always looking for ways he can use his money to make a difference in the lives of others. He loves to give, and it's such a blessing to be a part of it! And then there's my buddy Andrew. He had only $16 in his pocket when he left for a mission trip to Africa, but he had such an amazing experience and God used him. And Alex, I got to be a part of it—I got to encourage him to go and now he's encouraging me! He tells me about the people he met—how they have joy that isn't based in possessions. Just talking to him is a blessing! My life might be simpler than it used to be, but it's full! Helping others experience life is the biggest blessing in my life."

Scott looked as if he would explode with joy just talking about it. "Well, you do make a pretty convincing case for it," Alex finally said, unsure how to respond to such a passionate answer.

"That's part of the blessing!" Scott responded. "I get to share what living an abundant life is really like with you and with others."

Just then, Kerry appeared almost out of nowhere, coffee cup in hand. Alex and Scott were so deep into their conversation that they hadn't even noticed her come through the front door, although she had clearly been there long enough to get her coffee. "Is it too late to join in?" she asked, smiling at the two men.

"Not at all!" answered Scott. "How did you manage to sneak in here without us seeing you? We were just talking about what we want our lives to look like."

Kerry sat next to Alex who brought her up to speed. "I started to share our list, but I didn't get very far."

"Oh, good—I wanted to talk about that with you two anyway. Setting boundaries like these is a new thing for us, but we know that we need to, both for our kids and ourselves. Thinking about what we wanted for them helped us think of ways that we needed to change our own lives."

"That's a great way to look at it," said Scott. "Let's take it one step further, and think about this: When you die, what do you want your eulogy to say? Think about what would happen if people actually told the truth at funerals. If I had died ten years ago and someone told the truth about me at my funeral, they would have said, 'Scott really knew how to run a business, and he was shrewd with his money. He always got the best deal and his family always wished that he had the same passion for them as he did his business ventures.'" Scott looked from Kerry to Alex and smiled ruefully, shaking his head. "Can you imagine? But that's not what I wanted people to remember about me, so I had to make a change. I had to become the man I needed to be so that people would be able to say what I wanted them to say about me. Would you need to live differently than you do now so that those you leave behind would say the things you'd like them to say?"

"We'd definitely need to make some changes," admitted Kerry. "I'd want people to say that we were generous and kind—that we made others' lives better, but…"

"Like Kerry said, we'd need to make some changes. We *do* need to make some changes," said Alex with more conviction, looking at his wife.

"Like…?" prodded Scott.

"Well, like Kerry said before, we need to get to church more often, for one thing. But not just for the sake of going. We need, as a family, to actually *want* to have a relationship with God. We need to learn about Him and make Him a part of our lives. We really should go regularly."

"It's just hard because of Justin's soccer games— he has one most Sundays and a lot of them are in the morning," Kerry added.

"This is one of those times when you have to consult your vision to help you make a decision. Sometimes you just simply have to ask yourself the question, What's more important: his soccer games or going to church as a family?" asked Scott.

Alex sighed. "I know the right answer—it's church. But practically, it always seems more complicated."

This time, it was Kerry who challenged him. "Is it really more complicated, Alex, or would we just like it to be? Like when Justin tells me that he didn't have enough time to do his homework, but in reality, he spent the time he could have used for homework watching

TV, it's not complicated. It's just that his priorities were off. That's why I set boundaries that limit how much time he spends watching TV—because without them he doesn't do what's important. He wastes his time in front of a screen."

Alex didn't answer, but everyone at the table knew the truth. Finally Kerry put it into words. "It's not that we don't have time. It's that we haven't set the right boundaries because we haven't made it a priority."

Alex nodded his consent.

Scott agreed as well. "We have to set a lot of boundaries for our kids, too. Chris is on the basketball team and plays the drums, and Marie takes ballet lessons, but skipping church is never an option unless they're sick. And it's not as if this is some sort of punishment for them. They actually love going every week! It's a big part of their lives and that's intentional, but it wouldn't happen if we as parents didn't set the right boundaries for them. Without boundaries, it's hard to focus on what's important. So the question is, what do you say is most important to you?"

"Our family...though, I think I know where you're going with this," answered Alex.

Scott grinned. "You probably do. My point is, do your actions support your words? As you think about your vision, write down what you say is most important to you and use it as a guide to see if the way you're living demonstrates what you've written. Most of us have been taught to do what's right—we know what we need to do, but we either fail to follow through or we do it in the wrong order. We take steps that we think are good for us and our families, but since we're playing by the rules of the world, we never win."

"And to win, we need to play by a different set of rules," Alex added on cue.

"Exactly! If you're playing by the same rules as everyone else, you're playing the wrong game."

Alex stared into his coffee cup. It all made sense, and he wanted to get on board, but his brain hurt. This was a lot like trying to retrain a crooked tooth. "I'm starting to know the right answers, but living this out is going to be hard. I have so many bad habits to break."

"It does take time to change your habits," Scott admitted, nodding his head. "And I still need refreshers—that's why I go to a Lifeonaire retreat once a year for a tune-up. I first learned about how to set myself up to win by coming up with a Lifeonaire vision at one of these retreats, and every time I go I feel refreshed and encouraged. Actually, I'm heading to one next month. How would you like to join me? It's just three days, and trust me, those days can impact you for the rest of your life. Take what you're working on now with you there, and you will leave with a much clearer vision for your life and then the boundaries get easier."

· · ·

It was the morning of the second day of the Lifeonaire retreat, and Alex was having a lot more of those finding-his-feet moments. He plopped down on a bench outside the hotel and saw Scott approaching just as he settled back.

"Mind if I join you?" Scott asked, gesturing to the bench.

"Not at all, have a seat."

Scott sat and turned to his friend. "So what do you think?"

"I'm feeling a little bit of everything all at once, to be honest with you! It's great to be around others who are trying to live by the same goals that I am, but I have so far to go! It's encouraging to see how some people have changed their lives, but it's discouraging when I think of all the steps I need to take because I didn't do it right the first time. There are so many ways I want to use my money that would help me focus on living an abundant life, but I know I need to get rid of debt first. I don't want to have to wait on those things, but I know I need to."

"What kinds of things are you thinking of?" asked Scott.

"Well, I already told you how we'd like to give to others...but there are still things I want for myself, too, and I struggle with wanting all of these things. For the longest time I've wanted a boat, and I sometimes beat myself up because I thought I would have had this dream boat of mine by now."

"Why do you want a boat?"

"I just knew you would immediately start with the philosophy behind all of this." Alex teased. "What do you mean why do I want a boat? I want it for the same reasons anyone would. It would be so much fun, wouldn't it? Think about it... the open water, friends and family hanging out, having fun. It would be a blast!

I've had this as a goal of mine for about as long as I can remember. I even know the exact boat I want to get."

"Ok, that *might* be a good thing. The clearer your vision is about what you really want, the higher likelihood of you actually being able to experience it one day. So, describe this ideal boat of yours. Tell me a little more about why you want it and what it would do for you." Scott suggested slyly.

"Well for starters, it's all white with the exception of some deep blue paint all across the bottom. Even the interior is all white, but it has blue stitching on the seats to match the trim paint. I've had this boat in my head for years!"

"Sounds nice."

"And I even know the brand and model. I want a 38 foot Sea Ray," Alex says, beaming from ear to ear, clearly picturing the boat out on the water with him at the helm. "It kind of makes me mad that I work so hard but I'm still not to a point where I can buy one yet."

"I wonder how much something like would cost," questioned Scott.

"Well, that's part of the problem, Scott," Alex replied, "I have quite a few things like this in my vision, and it all costs money. I tend to like expensive things and it makes it really hard to accomplish everything I want to accomplish. It seems like everything costs so much money! This boat alone would cost more than a half a million dollars, and that's only one small aspect of my vision. There's a lot more than just this on there. I'd like to be a pilot someday too, maybe even own my own plane, but..."

"Hold on for a minute," interrupted Scott. "Let's just start with one thing at a time. What is it about this boat that you're so attracted to? What I mean is, why does it have to be a 38-foot boat? Why not get a 40-foot boat instead?"

"Well, that's true… I guess I *could* get a 40-footer. That would be even nicer!" Alex said, mentally revising his plan with this upgrade.

"Conversely, what about a 36 foot boat?" Scott questioned. "Could you get one of those and maybe save a little bit on the amount you'd have to come up with? That might help you get to this one aspect of your vision a little sooner, wouldn't it?" Scott looked at Alex with his eyebrows raised.

"Actually, you're probably right," Alex nodded. "For some reason I've been stuck on getting the 38-foot boat. I've wanted this for so long now that I'm not sure why it had to be a 38-footer, but I guess I could change it up a bit."

"When was the first time you ever wanted a boat like this? Can you even remember?"

"Oh yeah, I sure can. I'll never forget it!" Alex beamed, thinking back to a time when he was only 21 years old, having one of the most enjoyable weekends of his life. "A good friend of mine, Jason McMahon, invited me to go down to the lake with him and a buddy of his whom I'd never met before. Apparently, Jason's buddy had a really nice boat and was kind of a 'more the merrier' type of guy. Everyone called him "The Tank" although I'm a little embarrassed to say I can't even remember his real name. We ended up spending three full days together down on the lake on this guy's boat. It was a blast! There must have been 15 people on the boat over the course of that weekend. Even though I didn't know anyone except Jason when we got there, by the end of the three days together it seemed like we were all old friends. It was like one big never-ending good time and I didn't want it to stop!" Alex had a huge grin on his face. "It was the ultimate freedom!"

"And what was it about that, specifically, that you enjoyed so much?" asked Scott. "I realize you had a great time and I'm not trying to sound all philosophical on you. But was it the boat itself that made you have such a good time? Or was it something else?"

"I guess the boat had something to do with it since that's what we were actually doing for three days, but when I really think about it, what was so much fun was the people that were there. I had a great time getting to know everyone. It was as if none of us had a care in the world for those three days together."

"Interesting," said Scott. "Go on… anything else?"

"Yes, actually. I remember seeing how everyone treated 'The Tank.' They were all high fiving him all weekend, thanking him over and over again for being invited on the boat. Tank was one of the most fun guys I've ever met in my life. I still to this day don't know what he does for a living, but he was the perfect image of having 'made it' because everyone that was there just loved him."

"And that made you want to own a boat of your own someday? So you could be like Tank? Why do you think that is?" asked Scott.

"As ridiculous as this sounds, everybody loved Tank. You couldn't help but love the guy. I mean, here I am, an outsider, a stranger, and not only did he allow me to be on his boat for three full days, he also paid for everything for everyone there. It was awesome! I would love to be able to have that much money to where I could do that and not worry about how much everything was costing me."

"So is it safe to say that you really looked up to Tank because he was so loved by all of his friends?"

"Not only was he loved by all of his friends, he was loved even by the people that had just met him too! I didn't even know him very well and already had a lot of love for the guy! I remember Jason and I joking around that weekend that Tank was sort of the *'supplier of fun'* for everyone. He seemed to get a tremendous amount of joy out of seeing everyone else having such a good time. And the cool thing is, he's the one that provided all of that for everyone. So, yes, in that sense I looked up to him a lot. I think perhaps I've wanted to be more like Tank ever since that weekend because I want to be a part of helping others to have that kind of fun."

"So what I'm hearing is that you really want two things: to be the 'supplier of fun' kind of like Tank was to you, and you also want to experience the love of your friends, kind of like Tank felt with his friends that weekend." Scott asked, as if he already knew the answer.

"I think you just summed it up perfectly. Yes. I want that more than just about anything, only I'd like to do that with my family too. Back then I didn't have a wife and kids yet, so I want this for them as well." Alex replied.

"Would it be possible to accomplish these two things with a 36 foot boat instead of a 38 foot boat?"

"Well, I guess I could... I've just always had it in my head to get a 38 footer, and now that I think about it, it might have something to do with the fact that Tank had a 38 footer."

"Now you're on to something! This is the most important reason you're here this weekend! You see, your *vision* is that you want to be the supplier of fun for others. Your *vision* is that you want to experience the love of your friends. The boat, however, is just a vehicle, just one way for you to start living these aspects of your vision. Perhaps it's not the *only* way to live these parts of your vision though..." Scott was trying to stay on pace, knowing that the moments were counting down to Alex having a breakthrough that he'd also experienced just a few years earlier. "This part of your vision is crystal clear and I love that you want to provide so much for others, but if you think the only way you can experience those aspects of your vision is to *someday* save up a half a million dollars to afford a boat like this, you're doing the same thing most of the world is doing. You're postponing your vision until "someday." That someday may or may not ever happen, so in a way you're choosing *not* to live life now in hopes that you'll be able to some time in the future. The truth is, by taking this approach you may not ever get to experience this part of your vision. At the very least, you're postponing what you could be experiencing right now." Scott paused for a moment to let this sink in. "I'd much rather live my vision today, even if it meant using a different vehicle, than sit around and wait for it to someday *maybe* happen. Is having a 38-foot boat the only way you could experience these two aspects of your vision? Or would it be possible to live this part of your vision sooner in another way?"

"Hmm... I'm not sure. I've wanted this boat for so long. It would seem like I'm just settling if I were to give up that dream."

"Don't get me wrong, Alex, I'm not encouraging you to settle for anything! You don't have to give up on any of your dreams. And please don't think I'm suggesting there's anything wrong with having a 38-foot boat. I would just hate to see you postpone becoming your very own 'supplier of fun' and experiencing the love of your friends and family until *someday*. After all, isn't that what you've been doing all this time? You've wanted this boat for a long time, and you've worked long hours every week for years now, hoping that someday you could experience those things. But wouldn't it be great if you could have those same experiences, emotions, and feelings today?"

"Of course it would. For a minute there, it really felt like you were telling me I should downplay the things in life I really want. I've always been taught you should think big and when you do, the sky is the limit." Alex replied, unsure of what Scott was suggesting.

"What if you could find something other than the boat that gave you those exact same emotions and experiences and you could start experiencing these things in weeks or months instead of years?"

"Ok, I'm all ears," Alex replied, curious.

"Let me give you an example and perhaps this will make a lot more sense. A good friend of mine went through a similar situation a few years ago. His story was almost identical to yours, except that what he really wanted was a big vacation house in the mountains. He too was beating himself up about the fact that he'd gotten so far along in his life without having accomplished his goal. When I started to question him about his vision, I discovered what exactly it was about the vacation home that he really wanted. He wanted, more than anything, a place for him and his two boys to stay where they could go hiking and fishing and simply get away from everything. At the time, his boys were eight and twelve years old, and he was worried that if he didn't buy the vacation home soon, it wouldn't be long before they were too old to even *want* to do stuff like that with their dad any more. As a matter of fact, he wanted this vacation home so badly that he'd already gone out and gotten an approval on a loan to begin building one. I asked him why he had done that, if his vision mentioned anything about wanting to go into debt." Scott chuckled and Alex joined him. "Of course it didn't, however, the thought of actually buying a vacation home like this and paying cash for it didn't seem realistic to my friend. He thought about it, and quickly realized that without borrowing money to acquire the home it would take years before he could afford the vacation home he really wanted, and he truly felt like he just didn't have that kind of time."

Alex jumped in, "This is exactly what I struggle with! If I wait until someday when I can pay cash for everything, I'll be 100 years old before I get to enjoy life. My kids will be grown and have their own families by then."

"Yes, it would seem that way at first," Scott agreed patiently, "but when I dug a little deeper, I found out that this gentleman was also an incredibly spontaneous kind of guy who loves to experience new and different things. He gets bored doing the same thing over and over again, and so do his kids. The one thing they all loved about the outdoors is that they get to explore the woods and feel like little boys again. What excited him the most was experiencing new and different places all the time, so do you think he would have really been happy with a vacation home that he felt obligated to go back to every single time he and the boys wanted to get away? After all, if he was making a payment on a custom-build vacation home every month, why would he go someplace else, right?" Scott was sharing this story much like an experienced father would teach his son to tie his shoes for the first time.

"Ok, I get it… In this case, the vacation home probably would have been a perfect fit for about 6 months, but after the newness wore off, he would have probably been bored with it." Alex replied.

"That's right, but he would have been stuck paying for it for another twenty nine and a half years!" Scott answered. "And it's unlikely he would have had gone on vacation anywhere else since he would have felt a certain sense of obligation to go the vacation home he was already paying for each month. Not only that, but he would have had to work extra hours in his business to make the money required for the payment, the upkeep and all of the other things that need to be handled when owning property. While the vacation home seemed to be the answer to his vision, it actually would take him further from his vision. What he wanted was time with his boys, and this home would have taken more of his time than he'd ever considered."

"So, what did he do then, just settle for not ever getting his dream house?" Alex asked.

"Not exactly," Scott replied. "First things first, I told him we've got to get down to the basics again and simplify. In his mind the vacation house was the answer to his problem, but what he was missing was that the vacation house was just a vehicle, just *one way* for him to live out his vision with his sons. Unfortunately, that one way came with a lot of additional consequences that didn't necessarily fit his vision too, so I started asking him a series of different questions which helped him see a new perspective. The first thing I asked him was whether or not there was a way he could spend time fishing and hiking with his sons without actually *owning* a vacation home. The answer was an obvious yes. He told me that he could, of course, go out and rent a cabin for a couple of weeks. This solution wouldn't cost him anywhere near as much money as it costs to own a vacation home. With a vacation home, he would have had property taxes, insurance, maintenance costs and a whole lot more in addition to the actual cost of the house itself. With a rented cabin he could go enjoy his time, not have to worry about cleaning it when he got there, cleaning it when he left, or any maintenance or upkeep either. Not only would it be a lot cheaper for him to rent a cabin, it would also fit his vision better anyway, since now he would never be forced to go to the same cabin twice. He and his sons could be free to stay in different cabins all over the country and experience new places together. This would still give him what he wanted, which was the time with his boys, and it would fit his need for variety. Not only that, but since he loves to be spontaneous, he found out he could usually get a better deal by booking these little trips last minute, since a lot of cabin rentals will reduce their rates at the last minute if they have multiple vacancies.

"Wow, that makes sense. I'll bet he was thrilled to hear all of this!" said Alex, getting a little more excited about his own situation.

"Actually, he was only partially excited, maybe even a little depressed," Scott grinned at the memory. "The truth is, even though this new idea of renting a cabin was going to be a whole lot cheaper and more con- venient than buying a vacation home, he still wasn't in a position to be able to afford a trip like this financially. Even though this way was considerably less expen- sive than owning, it was still outside of his budget at that time."

"That's pretty scary considering he was just about to go out and get a big loan to buy a place! So I'm guess- ing you guys came up with a new set of financial goals to make enough money to be able to afford the trip at a later date then?" Alex asked.

"Nice try, but not quite! That's what the world would have told him to do, but instead, I simply asked him another question." Alex and Scott both laughed. Alex had learned early on that Scott very rarely gave a direct solution to any of his problems, and instead just asked a lot of thought-provoking questions. "I asked him if there was another way he could have these experiences right away, even if it meant he wasn't able to afford to rent a cabin. After he thought about it for a few minutes, he came to the realization that he could, if he wanted to, just take his sons on a camping trip instead of bearing the cost of a cabin. At first, it kind of seemed like he was downgrading his dream, but after he actually went out and did this with his boys, he admitted that it was one of the best experiences he'd ever had with those two young men. He told me after he'd gotten back that he couldn't believe he'd put off this part of his vision for so long. They had the time of their lives, it cost him next to nothing, and the best part of it is, he got to experience that in days, not years or decades. I never saw him so happy!"

"Ok, that makes a lot of sense." Alex replied, nodding thoughtfully. "Maybe instead of being stuck on buying a 38-foot cruiser boat, I could just go out and get a smaller little ski boat or a jet boat or something like that, something I could afford right now. Granted, I won't be able to fit 15 people on it, but I could still take a few friends and family out on the lake and have a great time! If I can put my ego to the side for a little

while, I'd bet I could have a really good time with everyone on a smaller boat and still experience that love we
were talking about earlier, *and* I could be the supplier
of all that fun!"

"That's a great plan, Alex!" Scott said encouragingly.
"And certainly a step in the right direction, but since
you're also wanting to get out from underneath of your
current debt load, what if we took this whole boat thing
one step further? Let me ask you a question: Do you
consider yourself an every day 'boater' type of guy?"

*Seriously? Another question? Just when I thought I had
it figured out... where's he going with this now?* "I'm not
sure. What do you mean by that?" replied Alex.

"I mean, let's be really honest for a minute. How
many times per year, assuming you had a boat like this,
would you want to use it? Would you say you would use
it thirty or forty times per year? More? Less?"

"Well I haven't really put that much thought into it
before. Why do you ask?"

"I'm just curious. Where we live, it's nice and warm
boating weather about six months out of each year. Are
you the type that will be out on the boat every day the
weather is nice? Or are you more the type that would
like to enjoy the boat on the weekends every now and
then?" Scott asked.

Alex replied, "I guess I never really put a number to
it before. I'm certainly not the type of guy that would
do it every day. Don't get me wrong, I like it and all, but
some people are just die-hard 'boat people' and that's
probably not me. I hate to say this out loud, but real-
istically, I would probably only go four or five times

per year. And I say that because there are a lot of other things in my vision that I'd like to experience too in addition to boating, and when I stop and think about it, there's just not enough time for everything."

"Ok," Scott replied. "Then why even bother owning a boat? Why not just rent one instead?" Alex just looked at him and Scott continued, "When you own a boat, there's maintenance costs, it takes time to get the boat titled each year, there are batteries to charge, insurance to pay for, storage fees, winterization, all kinds of responsibilities. But when you rent a boat, for as little as you actually want to use it, you don't have to worry about any of that stuff. When you want to go boating you simply make a phone call. They get the boat ready for you, they gas it up, they clean it up and they have it waiting for you on the dock, all ready to go. If anything goes wrong with it while you're out on the water, they'll come pick you up and get you another boat. When you own a boat, you do all that prep work yourself. Plus, when you're finished with a rented boat, you just hand them the keys and walk away. They clean it, they refill it with gas, they store it, and they pay for the upkeep and the insurance. You're done! And you still get to experience the love of your friends *and* be the supplier of fun. Why go out and spend all that money owning a depreciating asset that you're only going to use a handful of times each year when you can just rent one for the day or weekend and be done with it?" Scott looked at Alex, waiting for his response.

For the first time, the lightbulb in Alex's head was shining at full force. "Scott, I could actually do something like that this weekend! I mean, a boat doesn't cost that much to rent for the day, even for a whole weekend! I could afford that right now!"

"That's interesting, Alex. You mean to tell me you could actually start living parts of your vision today? What a concept!" They both laughed at the simplicity of it all. It was like a hidden picture puzzle, where the answer had been there all along, and all Alex needed to do was look at the picture in a new way to solve it.

Scott clapped his hand on Alex's shoulder and stood up. "We better get in there. The event is going to start back up in a few minutes and there's still a lot more to cover. This is just the beginning. You ready?"

"I'm ready. Let's do this!"

. . .

As Alex walked out of room on the final day of the seminar, he was exhausted and full of energy simultaneously. Reflecting on all he'd learned in recent weeks, he felt a new sense of direction. He wasn't exactly sure how he would get there, and truthfully, it still seemed a long way away to him, but for the first time in a long time, Alex felt like he was at least going in the right direction.

"I have to admit, just a few months ago I would have thought it to have been a complete waste of my time to go to a seminar like that," Alex confided to Scott as they walked down the long hall toward the hotel lobby. "I'm glad I went. Thanks for pushing me to go... and

I'm sorry if I fought you on so much of what you were trying to help me through."

"No problem," replied Scott, smiling at his friend. "I felt the exact same way as you when I started this whole process. I think fighting it is pretty natural. That's why we Lifeonaires call it *messing people up!*' I think God works in mysterious ways and I thank Him every day that He opened my eyes. It's actually not in my nature to want to keep things simple. I can really overcomplicate things if I don't stay true to my vision and keep it in front of me constantly. Even now, as much as I think I know and as far as I've come, I continue to learn what it means to be a Lifeonaire every single day."

"It's so ironic to me how complicated I've made things over the years." Alex said, shifting his Lifeonaire workbook from his left hand to his right. "I wish I would have known all of this about ten years ago." The men entered the lobby and sat down at a small table in the lounge area to continue their conversation.

"I hear you," replied Scott, chuckling. "The key to making this stick once you begin to understand your vision, is to make sure the steps you take don't include a bunch of negative side effects. In other words, as badly as you want something in your vision, like a boat, the last thing you want to do is end up becoming a slave to it because it conflicts with another area of your vision – like being debt free. I'll admit, it does take a little bit of planning... unless you want to live like the rest of the world, in which case you don't have to do any of this. But, if you want to live an outstanding life, it takes a plan. The sad thing is that most people spend more time planning a weekend getaway than they do their lives. They can spout off what they want their 401(k) to look like but can't tell you what they want their lives to actually look like."

"I definitely fell into that category," admitted Alex.

"Hey, I did, too. Most of us go about life the wrong way: we build our businesses and careers and then try to fit life into what's left over. The problem is that usually there's *nothing* left. Lifeonaire teaches us how to design our personal lives first. *Then* we can build our businesses and careers to fit the vision for our life. That way, we can experience life now, and not years down the road if our careers or pocket books allow us to. Rather than just setting a goal, which may or may not even get you what you really want, this approach is sort of like starting with eternity and working backwards."

"I hear you, Scott, and believe me, that's what I want," Alex stated with conviction. "It's just that taking the steps to change my life—my family's lives—can be a bit overwhelming." *That's an understatement,* Alex thought, looking down at his workbook and thinking about all he had written in it over the past few days.

"I know it is—I've been there, remember? How about we take a look at how to make a few areas of your life serve your vision rather than the other way around?" Scott suggested. "For example, if your motivation is an abundant life like you say you want it to be, what did your ideal life schedule look like?" he asked.

During the seminar, Alex was given the task of assigning his vision to a calendar, as though he were actually living that life today. This was a difficult exercise for him because as he filled in each time slot for his vision of life, he realized how vastly different his real calendar looked in comparison.

"I'd work a lot less, that's for sure—maybe half as much," Alex began. "I like what I do, but I don't want to do it nearly so much—that's why Kerry and I talked about setting boundaries about me not working on Sundays and not working every night. I'd have time to spend with my wife and kids. I'd eat dinner with them each night, and I'd go to Justin's games. I'd have time to volunteer, too."

"Speaking of dinner, wanna grab a quick bite to eat before heading home? We both have a bit of a drive ahead of us, and I'd hate to see you drive away on an empty stomach!" Scott teased.

"Sounds good to me" Alex replied. "It's not like we were running laps in the seminar, but for some reason I'm starving! I could eat a horse!"

They continued talking over dinner, looking at how to design life according to Alex's new vision—how much it would cost, but not simply how much it would cost in terms of dollars. Instead, they started to really look into how much *time* it would take to live out a vision like what was now on paper. They had to look into how much time he wanted to spend at work and with his kids, and how he'd design his business with the focus of the business being to fund his vision rather than what he had done in the past, which was to put the business first. Alex started to see that his business should have been designed to support his vision and the vision for his family financially, but not at the expense of the time he was able to spend with them. Alex, though exhausted, was exhilarated as they went over the ways he was running his business and his budget, and how they would need to change.

"Every business has its ups and downs," Scott shared. "The key is to base your budget and lifestyle on the down times. The up times are like a bonus and provide extra income. They're not there so that you can find additional ways to spend the money, but so that you can build the wealth you're seeking—the kind that will help you lead an abundant life."

"I've definitely missed that so far," admitted Alex. "It's always been so easy to build my life on the up times because once I found ways to step up my lifestyle to spend the extra money, I didn't want to go back. I don't want to slip into that habit again."

"That's why you need an action plan. If you want your life to look different, you need to do things differently than you have in the past, and that requires having a plan to stick to. You can't expect things to change if *you* don't change. If you make excuses and don't actually take the steps to do things differently, you'll still be in the same place, no matter what you say your intentions are."

"So that means I just need to make time for Justin's camping trip next week, no excuses. He'll be so excited." *And so will Kerry*, Alex thought with a small smile.

Scott nodded and opened his mouth, but a phone call on his cell interrupted before he could say anything. "Excuse me, Alex. This is one of my coaching students. I'll just be a minute."

Coaching students? Coaching what?

Scott answered the phone and told the mystery person on the line that he was in the middle of a meeting and that he would call them back when he got on the road. After a long pause of intent listening, with a huge grin on his face, Scott said, "Wow, congratulations! I'm so proud of you! You followed through. No one ever said it was going to be easy, but was it worth it? That's the question!"

Just then waiter came with check in hand. "Here you go guys, you can pay at the front counter whenever you're ready," and walked off as quickly as he came.

"I can't tell you how excited I am for you! Just think, now you can spend all of that extra money on anything you want." Scott said into the phone. "What's it feel like to be a free man?... Listen, I want to hear all about it and I also don't want to be rude to the gentleman I'm here with, so I'll call you back just as soon as I get in the car, okay? You got it.... You're welcome... But it wasn't all me, you're the one that executed the plan... Congrats again... I'll talk to you in a few... Bye."

"That sounded like a good phone call..." Alex prompted as Scott hung up, hoping to find out what all the 'congratulations' was all about.

"It was an excellent phone call, my favorite type of call to get!" replied Scott cheerfully. "I'll get this one," he said, reaching for the check. "You can get the..."

"No, *I'll* get this one. You can get the next one and we'll go someplace way more expensive!" Alex said, interrupting Scott with his own favorite line before he could get the words out.

"Thanks buddy. I appreciate it." Scott was beaming from ear to ear. Both from the free meal and the mystery phone call. "You know, nothing makes me happier than seeing someone living their vision and honoring God in the process."

"May I ask what that was all about? Or am I being too nosy?" asked Alex.

"Not nosy at all. That was a gentleman I've been coaching and consulting with for quite some time now. After three years of hard work, prayer, and honoring his vision, he is now officially debt free. I was congratulating him on becoming a free man!"

"Coaching and consulting... so that's where you make all your money!" Alex guessed, attempting to tease the truth out of Scott. "Running these seminars over coffee?"

"This is my fun business," Scott answered, smiling. "I do a number of other things, but this I do because I enjoy it. To finish up with what we were talking about, though, I expect you to be on that camping trip. Make time for it, and see what happens! I've got a bit of a drive so I'm gonna run. Thanks again for dinner."

"Any time. Thanks again for giving me the friendly push I needed to attend the seminar." Alex added. "I wish Kerry could have been here. We have *a lot* to go over together."

· · ·

Alex, Justin, and a dozen other men and boys made their way to the campfire after setting up their tents and getting situated in what would be their homes for the weekend. Justin immediately grabbed a hot dog and crouched by the fire to roast it, and Alex settled back into his camping chair and into his thoughts. He never could have predicted how the past few months had impacted his life...how they had impacted his entire family. He replayed everything in his mind, from the time he'd first met up with Scott to the past weekend at the Lifeonaire conference. Things had changed so much since then...a couple months ago, he would never have guessed that he'd be sitting here with Justin on his camping trip. And yet, here he was, getting to know his son better and spending an entire week away from work.

He felt a tap on his shoulder and turned to see Scott standing behind him with the man from two tents down. Alex stood to say hello as Scott made the introduction.

"Alex, meet John. John, this is Alex, a friend of mine. He has a deal he'd like to discuss with you sometime, and I promised him that I'd introduce you to him."

This is it! The moment I've been waiting for! Alex swallowed heavily, trying to remember what he'd wanted to say. And yet, talking to John seemed like a goal from a lifetime ago...

Alex extended his hand. "Nice to meet you!" He smiled at both men. "But actually, that deal no longer fits my vision—I'm passing on it."

Scott beamed with delight at the growth that he now saw in Alex, and John, who had been pursuing his Lifeonaire vision for a couple of years himself, seemed to know exactly what had just taken place. He grinned widely and shook Alex's hand.

"Alex, has Scott ever invited you to participate in our Tuesday night group?" he asked. "I think you'll find your journey a whole lot easier if you spend time with others who are also pursuing Lifeonaire lifestyles. It's made all the difference in the world for me."

"Actually, he did invite me about a month ago, and I have never made the time to get there, but now that it's part of my vision, I plan to be there regularly."

The men spent the rest of the night enjoying the company of the boys, knowing that they would have plenty of opportunity in the future to get to know each other better.

. . .

Alex pushed the front door open. "Kerry! Heather! We're home!"

"Alex!" Kerry rushed down the stairs and embraced him. She lingered for a moment before scooping up Justin in a hug as well. "So, how was it?" she asked her son, as Heather ran in from the playroom and leapt into Alex's arms, squealing in delight.

"It was awesome!" Justin exclaimed. "We cooked over the fire and went canoeing, and Dad even showed me some constellations! We barely slept at all!" He continued to recount the whole trip excitedly, going through each and every activity in excruciating detail. Alex nodded in wide-eyed, beyond-tired agreement, holding his little girl tightly in his arms.

Finally, Justin and Heather scurried up the stairs to his room to take a look at the pictures he'd taken, and Kerry turned to Alex and raised her eyebrows. "So how was it, really?"

That's a loaded question! "It was great! Exhausting, but great! It seems so ironic to me that just a few months ago I would have passed up this entire experience just so I could try to get some more work done." He smiled tiredly at his wife and reached out to hug her again.

This is abundant life, Alex thought, feeling Kerry's arms tighten around him and squeezing her back. *It's like Scott said: the greatest inheritance I can leave for my kids isn't a large estate—it's teaching them how to live. If I don't teach them the source of life and how to pursue it, no amount of money will ever make them happy. I've got to teach Justin—and Heather, as she gets older—how to master money and master life. If they can do that, they won't need my money, anyway. And if I don't teach them how to master these things, any money they got from me wouldn't really be a gift. Without knowing how to handle it, they'd just make the same mistakes I made.*

I'm not going to let them make those mistakes—if I don't do anything else in my life, I need to show my children true freedom. And I'm going to start with my own life—I'm going to show them what an abundant life looks like, not just from the worlds perspective but from God's perspective. I have so much to do... and I can't wait!

Epilogue

Three Years Later

Alex loaded the last case of diapers into his trunk and shook his head in amazement. Who'd have thought he'd be buying these things again? The looks on those mothers' faces were worth it, though. They'd started by "adopting" a single mother they'd heard about at church, providing her with enough diapers for her infant son every week. Lindsay, the young woman they were providing for, was struggling to make ends meet while raising her baby on her own, and had turned to her church for help. Alex and Kerry not only felt called to help her, they also got a tremendous amount of joy from being able to comfort Lindsay through one of the most challenging times of her life. Nowadays, they were providing diapers for three moms, and they could easily see themselves adding more to the list in the not-too-distant future.

"Are you sure this is going to be enough?" Kerry asks sarcastically, teasing Alex as he hopped on top of the trunk to get it to latch.

"Well, at least we don't have to be the ones to change all these diapers once their full of... you know... stuff!" Alex joked. "Thank God for that!"

At first, they weren't sure how much of a difference such a small thing could make, but seeing the looks on those mothers' faces erased all doubt. Alex and Kerry had never known what it was like to struggle to provide for their kids' needs, at least not like that, and seeing firsthand how much impact such a small gift could make had been a real eye-opener. They'd also never imagined that giving such a simple gift could bring them so much joy. And the best part was that they weren't only giving diapers to these young families—they also got to share about the life that God offered and tell them that it was God who was providing, through them.

Three years ago, doing something like this would have seemed like a chore. Of course Alex had wanted to give before being introduced to Lifeonaire, but in the past he would have rather just stroked a check because time was his enemy. Giving was more of a task to check off on his to-do list rather than something he had any true desire to get involved in. If someone had even mentioned driving a car full of diapers over to a total stranger's house, Alex would have thought it to be a complete waste of his precious time. He realized now that this was because he simply didn't have any time to spare back then. He was so busy working, trying to get ahead, that he never even had time to enjoy the life he was so busy creating.

"Have fun, tell Lindsay I said hello!" Kerry said as she leaned over the trunk to give Alex a quick but thorough kiss. "And try to get home soon if you can. Tonight is barbeque night and you run the grill *way* better than I do."

"I shouldn't be long," Alex replied, hopping down. "God knows we don't need the back yard catching on fire again like the last time *you* were in charge of the grill!"

"Uh-huh..." Kerry replied, narrowing her eyes at him in warning. "Keep it up and you'll be stuck eating charcoal briquettes as a side dish instead of the twice baked potatoes I'm putting in the oven when I get home." She tossed her head and smiled, clearly feeling as though she won this round.

"Ok, I take it all back!" Alex held up his hands in mock surrender. "You're the best wife *ever* and I love you more than anything... even if you *do* happen to be a pyromaniac who likes to burn down entire neighborhoods!" Alex smiled and pulled his wife close for another kiss. They smiled at each other, knowing that if anyone else heard this conversation, they would both sound crazy.

How far they'd come in only three years! Alex thought. One of the hardest decisions Alex and Kerry made as they started their Lifeonaire journey was the decision to sell their house. After all, they decided, as much as they loved living in that big monster of a house, there were chains that came with it. Not only was it a lot of square footage to maintain and clean, there was a pretty large monthly payment attached. They decided to go against the grain and actually rent a smaller place for a while, just to see if God would show them what to do next.

At the time, they were unaware of just how big of a blessing the decision to sell would turn out to be.

Especially since it was the exact opposite of what their accountant (and just about everyone else in their lives) advised them to do.

"Why would you sell your biggest tax write-off and rent a house instead? That's the worst thing you could possibly do from a tax perspective!" exclaimed Alex and Kerry's accountant in amazement.

"Why would I spend $1.00 in interest just so I could save $0.33 in taxes?" Alex asked back. This Lifeonaire stuff was truly starting to set in.

Kerry had a hard time with the move at first too. After all, moving meant leaving the custom-designed kitchen that she and Alex had spent months planning and renovating. There was also the pool in the backyard and the 'vacation-like' feel they spent so much time creating with all of the landscaping they'd invested in just a few years earlier. Although Kerry knew there were aspects of the old house that she was really going to miss, she also knew that none of those things compared to the desire she had for time with her family. Although she hesitated to sell the house, once she realized it would mean more time with Alex, the decision wasn't hard at all. After all, even the pool – as nice as it was – took a lot of time just to maintain. That huge yard took a lot of time to mow. The landscaping not only took a lot of time to maintain, it also cost a small fortune to keep it looking as nice as it did. Now that they were renting, they didn't have to take care of any of these things. If something needed maintenance, they called the landlord and he came and took care of it. When the air conditioner stopped working last year, they made a phone call and the landlord delivered a new one the very next day. Not only was their rental cheaper, the neighborhood pool was a mere five-minute-walk down the street. Kerry was happy that she didn't have to clean the pool every day and the kids actually used the new community pool more because there were so many other kids there. And their new house was just perfect for what they needed. Granted, it wasn't the spacious 3,600 square foot house they had before, but there was plenty of space for everyone in the house and none of the space was wasted. With all of this extra time on her hands, Kerry was able to take a few art classes at the local community college, a hobby that she had almost forgotten about in her previous life.

My family is different, too, Alex reflected as he drove to Lindsay's apartment. Though at first Justin had balked at joining a different soccer league that didn't play on Sundays, he fit right in on his new team, and though he wouldn't admit it, Alex could tell that he was glad that his dad now showed up at all of his games. Naturally, the assistant coach is *supposed* to show up at all of the games! Alex could hardly remember the days when he couldn't seem to make time to be at his son's games, and he didn't even want to think about what life would be like if he had kept to his old schedule. These days, the whole family ate dinner together just about every night, and their kids were learning firsthand how to give and share what they had rather than holding onto it. Justin had even given his old shin guards to a kid at church who needed some, and he sold one of his guitars—the nicer one—so that he would have money to pay for the rest of his team uniform.

Actually, it was hard to think of an area of life that hadn't changed in the last few years. Alex's entire mind-set was different, especially the way he thought about success. His entire business changed. Not only did he have to make some tough decisions to cut many of the unnecessary expenses in his business, he also had to put some major boundaries in place regarding his working hours. This was hard for him at first and took some getting used to, but it also actually forced Alex to be more productive since he no longer allowed himself to work the sixty to seventy hours per week he had become accustomed to. This meant he had to learn to rely on the help of others rather than trying to run the entire show single-handedly. Surprisingly, he was actually making more money running his business this way. While Alex's gross income was now less than what it was just three years earlier, his net income after expenses was significantly more than ever before. Because of this, he was able to begin to retire his debts one by one. He was starting to have more and more options in his business as he got closer to being completely debt-free, and that light at the end of the tunnel was shining brightly now compared to just a few years earlier when it seemed impossible. He was still debating whether he wanted to stay small but profitable or to invest in growing the business, but for the first time in his life, Alex was excited about the future of his business. The bottom line was that he had options and they were all good—that was definitely something new. And thanks to less late night takeout dinners at the office, he'd lost a little weight and looked and felt better than ever.

Not only were his business expenses drastically reduced, with all of the personal decisions he and Kerry were committed to, their personal expenses were drastically reduced as well. Now, it was a whole lot easier to earn enough money each month to cover the bills since there were so many fewer bills to pay! If he earned more than he needed, he saw it not as an opportunity to get more but to give more of himself. Now that they'd sold off their two brand new expensive cars, they immediately started saving more than $1,000 per month in car payments alone. Instead of having expensive cars with payments, they paid cash for two nice used cars. Granted, they were a few years old and not quite as nice as what they had, but they were safe, they got even better gas mileage than what they had before, and best of all – no payments! And their insurance costs and personal property taxes went down considerably as well. All of these little decisions and changes added up quickly.

Alex even sold off quite a few of the toys he never had the time to use, including the '68 Corvette – but only after he and Scott restored it with Justin and some kids from church. Not only did it end up being a fun project to work on, it also was a great bonding experience for Justin and Alex. Plus, the proceeds of the car went to pay off the loans on the two 4-wheelers sitting in the garage. Alex had decided that the 4-wheelers were the few toys he was going to keep, only now, not only were they free and clear of monthly payments, he actually had a plan to use them rather than just having them sit there collecting dust. The first weekend of every month, Alex hosted '4-wheeling day' with their church, where kids from all backgrounds could come out and take turns riding 4-wheelers. John Robertson actually donated the use of a ninety acre parcel of land he owned to host the events. This not only provided an absolutely phenomenal time for the kids from church, it was also a great way for the kids to learn that it *is* possible to have fun and honor God at the same time – and it brought kids into the church that otherwise wouldn't have ever been in that environment!

He'd also been investing a little here and there— not huge amounts but enough to begin to make a difference. Plus, with the money they'd been saving on expenses and no more interest payments on loans, they actually put away a nice stash of money to go towards the purchase of a new home. If they kept on this path they would be 100% debt free and be able to pay cash for a home within the next year or two. Granted, it wouldn't be the home they lived in before, but now that they tasted this much freedom, Kerry and Alex didn't want to take care of a home that large again anyway. While that had been a great house, what they wanted now was a *home*.

Kerry was thrilled to have been able to quit her job as well. After a lot of thought, she decided that her number one priority was to be home with her daughter, and she and Alex took immediate action with their finances so that, before long, Kerry was able to spend each day with Heather. Time flew quickly, and Heather was now six years old and getting ready to start kindergarten. Although Heather couldn't even remember the days when Mommy went to work every day, Kerry and Alex knew they had made the right choice and could see the positive changes reflected in their little girl. Heather had turned into quite the daddy's girl these days, running to him for comfort any time she would fall down and scrape her knee, and Alex loved it. It was something he never got to experience with Justin and he was determined not to miss out on the early years with Heather, too. What a difference just a few years of Lifeonaire decisions had made!

Alex and Kerry were, without a doubt, still a work-in-progress, but they were growing in their understanding of what it meant to live as Lifeonaires as they experienced an increasingly abundant life, and they eagerly shared it with their friends. At first, their friends – and even their families – thought they were crazy. But thanks to the advice Scott gave them, Alex and Kerry had expected this and pushed forward regardless of what anyone else thought or even said about them. In the beginning stages of Alex and Kerry's new Lifeonaire lifestyle changes, as Scott predicted, the rumors started flying. Some people thought Alex and Kerry were hurting financially and this is why they had to sell their big house. Some people gossiped that Alex's business was failing. But nowadays, most of their friends were envious of the lives Alex and Kerry had created for themselves and their family. Very few of them had come out and admitted this yet, but it was obvious in the questions they would ask and the comments they would make.

You guys seem to have a lot more time and freedom these days, what are you doing differently?

You two act like newlyweds! What's your secret?

Must be nice to go on vacation as much as you do…

Do you ever work anymore?

How is it that you can take off the entire month of December to spend time with family for Christmas?

What are you doing when you spend so much time with your church?

How is it that you actually look younger than you did just a few years ago?

While many of their friends were hesitant (just as they had been at first,) it was great to see several of them begin to change their lives as well. Alex and Kerry's abundant life was growing and rippling out to bring them more joy than they'd ever thought possible. As a matter of fact, one of the biggest challenges Alex and Kerry had over the course of these three years is that they now had all of this free time on their hands and very few of their old friends could spend it with them. It seemed most of them lived their lives the same way Alex and Kerry used to live, too busy to enjoy life. Now that Alex and Kerry were free, they found themselves having to find some new friends to spend time with. It seemed as though the friends they had the most in common with these days were the new friends they'd met at the Lifeonaire events they'd been attending regularly. Not that there was anything wrong with their old friends, Alex and Kerry still loved them dearly.

They just knew that they also needed to be around others that were 100% committed to the Lifeonaire way of thinking if they wanted to continue down the Lifeonaire path. After all, so little of the world is living this way, it would be easy to get sucked right back into every day life again without this support.

Visions of the last three years flashed through Alex's mind as he pulled into the parking lot of Lindsays apartment to deliver her portion of the diapers.

"Hi Alex!" Lindsay said as she opened the door with her little boy in her arms. "Thank you so much for the diapers! You are a Godsend!"

"Looks like you have your hands full. Mind if I come in and drop these somewhere?" Alex asked with a smile at the baby.

"Please do. I'm just about to run out, so your timing is perfect," replied Lindsay. "If you don't mind, please set them right over there, next to the changing table."

As Alex crossed the living room, a young man came out of the kitchen carrying a baby bottle and said cautiously, "Alex? Are you the Alex that renovates houses?"

"Hey there," said Alex. "Yes I am. And you are…?"

"I'm sorry…" Lindsay said, joining them. "This is my brother, Sam. He comes over from time to time to help me out with the baby. With his work schedule, that equates to about once a year," Lindsay said jokingly. "Sam, how do you know Alex?"

"Work. I'm an electrician." Sam said, offering his hand to Alex. "I worked for the general contractor you used for the property over on Birdie Hills Lane a few months back. I don't think we've met, but I saw you a few times as you came over to check out the work we were doing. It's nice to finally meet you in person."

"Great to meet you too!" Alex said, "I'm sorry I didn't get a chance to meet you personally before. I let my general handle most of the details of our projects these days, and I do my best to stay out of his way. That project has been done for a while now... how have you been since?"

"I've been ok. Work has been pretty busy lately. There's so much construction going on that they've got me working a ton of hours right now."

"And how do you feel about working so many hours?" Alex asked, realizing that he almost sounded like Scott with his inquisitive questioning.

"It's kind of a love-hate relationship. I'm not afraid of hard work by any means but this is the first day I've had off in almost four weeks. Makes it kind of hard to come help Lindsay and do a lot of the things I need to be doing when I only get one day off every three weeks." Sam said, slightly embarrassed at how much he just divulged to a man he just officially met for the first time. "I'm sorry, you were just making small talk and I'm over here giving you my life story."

"Don't worry about it... I used to be just like you." Alex replied, "But we have to be careful about working too much, Sam. Even the Bible tells us we're supposed to have at least one full day of rest every week."

"Sam doesn't go to our church," Lindsay interrupted, rocking the baby on her hip.

"That's ok." Alex responded. "I didn't mean to get all 'churchy' on you, but anyway, I'm assuming that even though you're not afraid of hard work, you still don't want to *have* work that many hours, right, Sam?"

"You got that right," Sam replied quickly. "But I don't have much of a choice. Not only does my job require it, I need the money. That's why it's sort of a love-hate thing. I make good money doing what I do, and I can't really slow down because I need that money."

"I can relate..." replied Alex, nodding his head. "I used to do the exact same thing. I worked seventy or more hours a week, made a good amount of money but didn't have any time to enjoy it. Plus, I had lots of bills going out the door every month, so even though I was seemingly making a lot of money, I didn't have time to enjoy any of it. It was just never enough. It seemed like everything I made went towards bills and there wasn't much left at the end of the month for me to have any fun. Thank God those days are over. Thank God for Lifeonaire."

"*Life-uh-what?*" asked Sam, with a grin.

"Yeah, that's exactly what I was thinking... *Life-uh-what?*" asked Lindsay, and they laughed.

"Lifeonaire," replied Alex. "Sort of like the word Millionaire, only with a *life*. It changed my whole life – my business, my finances, my family – it changed *everything for me*."

"Ok, so what is this Lifeonaire thingy? Is it just for big business guys like you?" Sam asked.

"No, Lifeonaire is for everyone, not just big business owners. And you'd be surprised how small my business actually is, but that's not important right now."

Alex responded with a smile. "You really want to learn this stuff?"

"Are you kidding me?" Sam responded. "I'd do just about anything to stop working these crazy hours and start making millions of dollars like a Lifeonaire makes."

"Why do you want to make millions of dollars?" Alex asked, realizing that he *really* sounded like Scott now. "Wait... before you answer... I have got to get going because tonight is barbeque night at our house and I told my wife I wouldn't be long..."

"That's okay," Lindsay interrupted, throwing a look at her brother. "I'm sorry my brother is keeping you away from your family time. We didn't mean to..."

"Don't worry about it one bit." Alex jumped in. "I'm actually happy to help. I've been where Sam is. I just have to make sure I get back in time to help with the grill. I have an idea though... if you guys aren't busy, how would you like to join us? I could share with you some of the Lifeonaire principles over dinner if you are serious about wanting to know more."

"You would seriously do that for us?" Sam asked, taking off his ball cap and running his hand through his hair. "I'm sorry if I sound so eager, it's just... I wasn't expecting to even meet you today much less go to your house and hear from you how you struck it rich with all of your property renovations and projects." He looked from Alex to his sister excitedly.

"We clearly have a lot to talk about, Sam. You guys want to ride with me and I'll just take you back home later tonight? Bring the baby too, just as long as you know I'm happy to supply the diapers but I'm not so good at changing them anymore!" Alex chuckled at his own joke. "We'll have fun."

"Sounds good to me," said Lindsay.

"Me too!" said Sam. "Thank you for even offering!"

"I just have one condition…" Alex announced. "If you like what you hear tonight, and *only* if after hearing it you think it's something you want to pursue, I just have one request of you. The next time you get a day off, you allow me to take you to lunch at this little coffee shop that's near and dear to my heart. My treat."

"Are you kidding me?" Sam said, "That sounds like a deal that's too good to pass up! I can't even believe you're even offering this right now!"

"Don't worry," replied Alex, "If we meet up again after that, I'll let you buy and we'll go someplace *a lot* more expensive."

The three of them laughed as they gathered a few things for the baby and headed out the door.

• • •

The truth was, the last three years weren't easy. No one ever said becoming a Lifeonaire would be. But was it worth it?

It's like Scott said: We all need a Lifeonaire vision, and that vision should be focused on an abundant life and helping others achieve the same. Until recently, I never even had a vision at all. Having the right one that honors God and is in alignment with what He wants for my life is what has made all the difference. And the truth is, none of us are capable of doing this on our own. We need help. We need guidance. And we need more leaders in this world who are willing to step out and go against the grain of what the world teaches so we can be free to live life abundantly. I can either choose to be a part of the solution or a part of the problem. Today I choose to be a part of the solution. Today, I choose to live abundantly. Today I choose to live what I've learned by sharing with others. Today I choose to be a Lifeonaire.

Final Thoughts from the Authors

The story you've just read, although fictional, is an accumulation of hundreds of real life stories of real life people just like you and me. Almost every story in this book is a true story that has taken place either within the lives of Steve Cook and Shaun McCloskey, or has taken place within the lives of our students. Our challenge was narrowing it down and combining *so many* incredible stories into the lives of just a handful of characters within the book

We'd like to share with you just a few examples of real people that have been affected by the Lifeonaire message, omitting their names to respect their privacy. One particular couple comes to mind who were literally working 18+ hours per day, seven days per week. They had been working this schedule for a number of years. When we met them, although they were working hard every day, they were actually moving backwards, mere inches away from filing bankruptcy, nearly losing everything they had worked for over the previous ten or more years. These were not stupid people. They were incredibly smart business people who just a few years earlier seemed to have it all – a fast growing business, lots of money coming in every month, everything that much of America is seeking. But, like so many other stories, things changed. The economy changed, their business changed, and their debts overwhelmed them. In an effort to make good on their obligations, they worked more and more, but more was not enough. It was only when they created and began to understand their vision that things started to change. By attending Lifeonaire events and surrounding themselves with other Lifeonaires who encouraged (okay, almost forced) them to try some new approaches, I'm happy to report that today their business is completely different. Through hard work, dedication, and the support of other Lifeonaires, their financial needs are only a fraction of what they once were, and as a result, they now work fewer hours than ever before. This couple actually took nearly four months off this past year to travel much of the United States. For the first time ever, they are reading the Bible with interest, and have enough quiet time to sit and listen to God's word. They're seeing His work in their lives for the first time ever – and much of it comes down to having the quiet time to actually sit and hear it. Most people today are so busy that even if the clouds parted and the heavens above spoke to them personally, they wouldn't hear it. It would be drowned out by the constant bombardment of noise, information, and technology.

Another Lifeonaire student went from working a 60+ hour per week job as an engineer to becoming the CEO of his own company, now spending the majority of his time with his family. Although he loved what he did at his job, he also knew that he couldn't continue to stay at the company he worked for and be a good father at the same time. He barely saw his first two children since he was out the door headed to work by the time they got up each morning, and he got home each night just as they were getting in bed. They now have three children. His wife recently told us that their youngest child now runs straight to Daddy when he falls and scrapes his knee, something that neither of their older two children ever did when they were little. The first two always ran to Mommy instead. They didn't know Daddy very well, so why would they? They now spend the majority of their summers on their family boat, which *does* fit their vision. It's not a 38-foot Sea Ray, but it suits their needs for everything they choose to use it for.

Another couple restored their marriage after getting clear on their visions. The gentleman in their relationship came to us sharing that he gets home from work each day and goes off and does his own thing (more work, hobbies away from his wife, etc...) and his wife does the same thing. They had lost their passion for each other, and were spending more time doing things on their own than they were doing things together anymore. Once their vision got clear, they started taking steps to make their marriage a top priority again, and almost overnight, their entire relationship changed. Not only did this restore their marriage, it also overflowed into every other aspect of their lives as well. They even made more money as a result of their marriage being a priority.

My eyes tear up as I hear story after story like this on an almost daily basis.

Another Lifeonaire student lost more than 60 pounds in just a few short months as a result of his vision being clear. He realized for the first time in his life that the weight he'd put on wasn't who he really was. When the vision became clear, the "how to" was the easy part.

Another student went from being totally and completely bankrupt, losing his house to foreclosure as well as having his truck repossessed at his place of work right in front of his co-workers, to making more than one million dollars in net profit the very next year – all a result of having a crystal clear vision and a plan to get there – and all done working fewer hours than he had ever worked before.

Shaun McCloskey: When I think of my own life, I used to be forced to make tens of thousands of dollars every month just to meet my expenses (stage two needs) before ever getting to spend a dollar living my vision. This forced me to work many hours and I never felt free. I made a lot of money back then, but if I had a slow month or two in my business, it would take another 3-4 months to catch up again, which happened often. I was a slave to my business in every sense of the word. I thank God every day that I learned these lessons before I had children. I can't imagine working the same hours today as I did back then now that I have three kids at home.

Steve Cook had more than $4.5 million dollars worth of debt that was affecting not only his desire for freedom, it was also hugely affecting his ability to give. One of his greatest joys in the world is his ability to give. Yet each month, he had a choice to make. He could give, but not give too much, or he would become fearful that the following month he wouldn't be able to service his debts. By the way, that entire $4.5 million in debt is completely paid off now, and not by going out and filing for bankruptcy. He actually paid it all off—every last cent. Today, Steve's needs are very little, he lives a very simple life, and he gives more than he will ever admit to anyone. Today, Steve has joy – and it all started with a vision.

I could write an entire book just on the stories we have from our students. They are absolutely incredible and they are all true. And each time I think I've heard it all, I hear another one that brings tears to my eyes.

Since the time that Lifeonaire came into our lives, we've helped coach thousands of people from all walks of life. We've seen story after incredible story of miracles that have taken place in the lives of people that were once living as slaves to their debt, their work, their "stuff", and many other things that God never intended for us. While our work is important, it has unfortunately become the primary source of significance for most men and women in this country. We strive for things that we think will make us happy, when very few of us understand what will truly bring us joy and fulfillment. Most of the world today works harder than ever in an effort to buy things and live a life that will impress people we don't even know or care about. And we trade our lives in the process. Lifeonaire starts with understanding and creating a vision for your life that is not only congruent with what God intended for you to experience—a life of abundance—but also about living a vision that is in alignment with Gods' purpose for your time on this earth. While each of us may have been given a unique, individual purpose for our lives, the underlying reason for living our purpose is to make a difference in the lives of others.

Mark 8:36 So what does it profit a man to gain the whole world and forfeit his soul?

How can you get started?

Step One

Begin to develop your vision

Granted, this is something we teach at our Lifeonaire event over the course of three full days together, but even if you don't have all the steps right now, you can at least begin to make progress. Start by putting on paper what you would like your life to look like if you could have it any way you wanted. The point is, *get it on paper!* It does you no good having it all in your head since living your vision this way will change depending on your mood. Claim your free sample of a Lifeonaire vision at www.lifeonaire.com/bookdeal.

Step Two

Get Stage Two Needs Met

Begin to implement the Four Stages to Financial Prosperity, including getting your stage two needs met. If your stage two needs (expenses and cost of living according to your current lifestyle) are high, consider things you can begin to do to reduce them. What can you simplify which will help bring you closer to your vision *faster?* (Remember, we're not suggesting you give up things in life. Instead, we're asking you to consider whether or not some of the things you currently have in your life are truly enhancing your life and bringing you closer to your vision. A good question to ask is, "Is this expense in my life necessary to bring me closer to my vision *today?* Not someday, TODAY!") To get free teachings on the Four Stages to Financial Prosperity, go to www.lifeonaire.com/bookdeal.

Step Three

Get around other people
that are pursuing Lifeonaire

It's too hard to do this on your own without any support.

Go to www.lifeonaire.com and register your email address to get free updates/lessons/interviews about Lifeonaire.

To obtain the most current speacials for a Lifeonaire event, go to www.lifeonaire.com/bookcoupon RIGHT NOW and sign up for our next Lifeonaire event. It will change your life.

Step Four

Share Lifeonaire with others

Now that you've finished this book, please give it to someone you know that will read it.

Visit our website at www.lifeonaire.com and buy at least 2 more books to share with at least two other people that you care about. You have the option to send the book anonymously, if desired. Or share your perspective of what the book has done for you and why you felt it was so important to share a copy.

To obtain a free Lifeonaire discussion guide that can be used for personal study or for group discussion, go to www.lifeonaire.com/bookdeal.

Continue Your Experience With Lifeonaire

www.lifeonaire.com

1. Share your thoughts or questions about Lifeonaire on the forum.

2. Like us on Facebook at www.facebook.com/lifeonaire

3. Discuss the book and Lifeonaire principles with others

4. Communicate with Steve Cook and Shaun McCloskey, the authors

5. Read the Lifeonaire Blog

6. Purchase additional copies of the book as well as study guides

7. Find out about upcoming Lifeonaire events

8. Sign up for a complimentary subscription to the Lifeonaire newsletter

For information about having the author speak to your organization or group, please contact us at speaker@ lifeonaire.com

Special Offers From Lifeonaire

www.lifeonaire.com/bookdeal

www.lifeonaire.com/bookcoupon

Here's what others are saying about Lifeonaire events

J.P. Moses - President and Founder - REITIPS.com
Lifeonaire is a profoundly powerful concept... A real paradigm breaker in so many ways for me. I've been a part of it for the last 6 years. I Highly recommend their events. Lifeonaire is truly amazing stuff. I've been a student, fan and advocate for years now - these guys have really crafted something unique and powerful. It just keeps changing my life. I can't recommend it highly enough. Anyone who's not satisfied with "stuff" and money and has realized it's really about slicing yourself a bigger piece of LIFE, should do everything they can to make it to this shindig. I've been there 4 times now.

Cody Sperber - President and Founder - Clever Investor
Don't get me wrong...I was at a point in my life where I was "open" to hearing their message. I think this is very important if you are thinking about going. At the end of the day...only you can "act" on the ideas these two will share with you! If you have a chance to hear Shaun and Steve do their Lifeonaire training I highly suggest you go. I saw it a little over a year ago and it changed the way I thought about my business, making money, and the importance of family. As an entrepreneur we get so caught up in our businesses that we easily set aside the things in life that are really important. They do a fantastic job of laying out a gameplan of how you can "start living life to the fullest" while running a business.

For latest deals on events, visit www.lifeonaire.com/bookcoupon

Here's what others are saying about Lifeonaire events

Steve York
I have been going thru life setting goals and reaching some, getting distracted and jumping around, being satisfied for a little while then making wrong choices and not knowing why. Then I attended the Lifeonaire event and learned why. I have been making choices using the wrong criteria. What a revelation! Now I am building my life around a vision and it has nothing to do with how much money I can make. But on what my vision is and what will make me not just happy but satisfied, I am including my wife now more than ever and am "seeing" the end from the beginning. My choices are clear as I use the vision.

JFT
A big difference in Shaun's program and every other program that I have taken was that he didn't mention anything about selling "the next program" and he still has me craving for more. He is more concerned with his students success than making the next buck. I truly believe in his philosophy that if you help people succeed the money will come and he practices what he preaches. You can tell he actually cares about his students. I was in real need of something to help me to find direction in my life and the Lifonaire program was just what I needed. I have achieved more in the few weeks since the class than in the three months prior.

What people are saying about this book!

Jason W - Amazon Review
WOW! Told as a captivating fictional story, this book highlights and brings to light a number of principles and concepts that run completely counter to common knowledge. It tells us why so many of us have it all wrong and how we can fix our situation. It's hard to put into words what this book does to your thinking and perspective, but I can tell you you'll never look at money and life the same. It forces you to examine your own life and choices in ways that most people never get the benefit of doing. The insight is astounding. It's not a difficult read, but as profound as they come. Order this book today!

Keith.Borg - Amazon Review
This book is much more than the financial freedom books I've read in the past. This book read much like a fiction novel. Through a series of stories this book demonstrates how someone can refocus their life on what's truly important to them (e.g. family, friends, charity, lifestyles, etc). As the book progresses, the fictional character is led through a series of exercises and lessons around finances, time, and lifestyle that leads to a transformation of the character's life.

This book lead to some serious discussions between my wife and I on how we were spending our time and money. Through the exercises we were able to determine what life goals we wanted to focus on and work towards those. This is not a transformation that happens overnight but it very useful in developing a flexible map of where we want to go. It was definitely worth the read.

What people are saying about this book!

Scott - Amazon Review
When I ordered this book I had not yet heard anything about it. I originally saw it on Facebook. I thought it was a real estate book. I was initially disappointed when i Opened it to find it was a fiction book. I read a lot of business books but never read fiction. I started to read it at about 9:30 pm and stayed up until about 3:30 am to finish it. It was that good. It has really made an impact on my thinking and I am still thinking about this book daily and making the necessary changes. I was definitely pleasantly surprised as I had no expectations going into it. I highly recommend the book!

Gary S. Tretter - Amazon Review
This was a great book and it is changing the way that me and my wife are looking at our life. We have realized that we are just running in the rat race like everyone else and we want to start living our life the way we want to live it instead of the way the world thinks we should. I am very thankful that Steve wrote the book. It is changing our lives.

Dominic Drascola - Amazon Review
Authors Steve and Shaun have done a fantastic job putting together a fiction publication that, through and through, represents anything but fiction. Compiled from a plethora of real life stories from their own lives, and the lives of others, the lie of what the American dream should be according to a modern, liberal, care-free, debt-burdened U.S. society is exposed. The result is an eye-opening revelation which practically empowers anyone who is serious about taking charge of their lives. An absolute "must read" which immediately puts the reader at a crossroads of decision...take charge of your life and experience it abundantly or let your life be defined by circumstances as it just "happens" around you. PLEASE GET THIS BOOK! You will not regret it!!!!

Made in the USA
Middletown, DE
31 January 2017